To Julie —
All the best in your
future endeavors!
— Adriana

Career Sudoku:

9 Ways to Win the Job Search Game

Adriana Llames

First Edition

About the Author

"One of Chicago's Finest Career Coaches"
-Chicago Examiner

Adriana Llames is a veteran career coach with more than a decade of expertise working with C-level executives, mid-level management and administrative professionals alike. As a featured expert on top job search Websites such as TheLadders.com, she is known in the career industry for her depth of knowledge and ability to craft unique search strategies.

In addition to industry features and her book, *Career Sudoku: 9 Ways to Win the Job Search Game*, Ms. Llames developed a popular Webinar series called "9 Ways to Win the Job Search Game," which provides skills, tools and expert advice to all professionals. She is also the developer behind <u>HR In-A-Box</u>, a human resources software product that has been helping small businesses across America for more than 10 years.

Ms. Llames is a national speaker with her "9 Ways to Win the Job Search Boot Camp" seminar series, touring America and sharing with job seekers her search approaches, career transition success stories and networking strategies. She has been a keynote speaker and emcee for The Society for Human Resources Management, Colorado State University, Rotary International, Right Management (a Manpower Company), Drake Beam Morin Career Services, The American Society of Training and Development and more.

Ms. Llames holds a Bachelor of Science degree in business management and has completed more than 30 post-Bachelor courses in management, leadership, diversity and culture, including four from Harvard Business School's management leadership program. In 2007, she accepted an invitation to join the National Association of Women Business Owners and was awarded the Golden Goose Award by Franklin Covey Centers for Leadership.

To learn more about Ms. Llames, please visit www.adrianallames.com.

Acknowledgement

I will not attempt to cite all the authorities and sources consulted while preparing this book. To do so would require more space than available! The list would include departments of the U.S. federal government, libraries, higher education institutions, Web sources and many individuals.

I will acknowledge a few key people, however. Valuable information and inspiration was contributed by copyediting firm *Concise.Correct.* at concisecorrect.com—I'm forever grateful, thank you; Paula Ledbetter Sellergren of LedbetterPR.com for lending her brilliant public relations talents and keen design eye; Kristi with 2Face Design did a wonderful cover design; and Adam Agosto of getreadygraphics.com added the final touches to the typography, bringing *Career Sudoku: 9 Ways to Win the Job Search Game* to completion.

I sincerely thank these lovely people, and I know they're proud of their work and their contribution to the book community. A special thanks goes to Melissa Giovagnoli for her connections in the book community and to Brad Laney for introducing me to Melissa.

Most important, the support of my family, closest friends and the Starbucks "crew" has been instrumental in my pursuit of realizing this book from conception to fruition. Thank you for your love and patience during this process. I am grateful to have all of you in my life.

—Adriana

"To be a champ you have to believe in yourself when no one else will."
-Sugar Ray Robinson

Getting a job is a game, plain and simple. It's a structured, interactive pursuit in which there are numerous players, distinct goals, various rules, and exciting and difficult challenges. And this is a game you need to win because a lot is at stake. The good news is this: I'm going to give you everything you need to be a champion.

Forget what you *thought* you knew about job searching, résumés and interviewing; the game is played differently today. Now, you can get superior results from your résumé, land more interviews and network with greater efficiency, making your job search faster, easier and more fun. I'll let you in on information about how to create a résumé that gets results, how to naturally and confidently network, how to have an impressive interview and negotiate the right offer for your needs and wants. Yes, you can still negotiate in today's career landscape.

There are times during your job search when you'll want to give up. This game is tough. I know because for more than a decade I've coached clients looking for jobs, and I, too, have looked for my fair share of them. If finding a job was effortless then everyone would have one right now, there wouldn't be record rates of seekers and this book wouldn't need to be in your hands. You wouldn't need to find creative ways to tap into the "hidden" job market to land a position.

To be victorious, you need to market *you*—online, offline, and with a powerful, polished résumé. I began coaching with some of these methods 10+ years ago and the finale fell into place with *Career Sudoku: 9 Ways to Win the Job Search Game*. You will love it.

Why Career Sudoku?

Job searching today is a process that requires building a foundation of knowledge and crafting a strategy to get you from point A, job seeker, to point B, new hire.

In the game of Sudoku, there are only nine numbers and it takes a well-organized strategy to have all nine fit in each row, column, and region at the same time. The same well-organized strategy applies to the new game of job searching. Without a plan or roadmap, you will feel lost, frustrated and confused. With a plan, this game can be straightforward and even exciting. This system works if you work it, and you will find everything here you need to beat the competition.

Thank you for investing your time with me and allowing me to share my secrets to job search success.

Disclaimer

This book's information is sold with the understanding that the publisher and author are not engaged in rendering legal or other professional services. If legal or other expert assistance is required, the services of a professional should be sought.

It's not the purpose of this book to reprint information that is otherwise available to job seekers, individuals in career transition or recruiters; it's intended to complement, amplify and supplement other texts. (For more information, see the many references in the Networking Resources Appendix.) The purpose of this book is to educate, entertain and support people in their job search efforts. The publisher and author shall have neither liability nor responsibility for any person or entity with respect to any loss or damage caused or alleged to be caused directly or indirectly by information provided in *Career Sudoku: 9 Ways to Win the Job Search Game*.

Job searching is not always a quick or easy venture. Anyone in the process of transitioning from one position to another must expect to invest time and effort without any guarantee of triumph in the near term. Jobs do not find themselves and they do not find candidates by themselves.

People find jobs and people hire people. Finding a new job is about connecting with people.

Every effort has been made to make this book as complete and accurate as possible. There may be mistakes, however, both typographical and in content. Comprising information about job search strategies, techniques and tactics only up to the print date, this text should be used only as a general guide.

This one's for you, Mom.
Thanks for being you *and* allowing me to be me.

CHAPTER ONE

RESUMÉS THAT GET RESULTS

	9		6			3		
				8	3			5
2					7			
	8					5		
3							4	
	1							2
	7							
1			5		9		6	
	4		3			7		

"The typical hiring manager looks at a candidate's Resumé for 10 to 15 seconds."

-Tracy Levine, President, Advantage Talent, Inc.

What if you could send your Resumé off and feel confident that you just put your best foot forward?

Imagine hitting "send," sitting back, waiting for the phone to ring and then walking into an interview knowing your Resumé rocks.

According to Angela Jones of ArticleSnatch.com, employers reject 90% of Resumés they receive. That's a staggering number. Resumés can be boring, too long, too short, have too much information or too little.

The first way to win the job search game is to have a Resumé that gets noticed—one that gets results. Do you know what a written summary of your work is supposed to do? **A Resumé has but one purpose: to land an interview**. That's it. Nothing else. The key to having a Resumé that rocks is creating the perfect combination of length, information and presentation to *sell you*. We'll explore that later.

If you're a recent college graduate, congratulations! It's important to note that your job search game is unique, and your Resumé has some very special considerations. For specific tips tailored to your needs, please visit www.adrianallames.com.

Chapter 1.1 | It's All About You

Award-winning singer and songwriter Toby Keith says it best in one of his biggest hits: "I wanna talk about me, me, me, me, me." While he may be settled in terms of a job, Mr. Keith certainly still wants to talk about Mr. Keith. Take a hint from him and get ready to shine a spotlight on you. This is your one opportunity to focus entirely on the absolute best results you have generated over your entire professional career.

Chapter 1.2 | Resumé Raisin Bran

Your Resumé should only comprise information that will land you an interview. It doesn't get any more clear-cut than that! Let's focus on what information you should be highlighting.

Picture yourself walking through the cereal aisle at your local grocery store and you have a goal to eat less sugar and carbs. You see a new Kellogg's Raisin Bran box that says "Less Sugar, 10g Carbs, Great Flavor" in the middle of the healthy cereal section. You look at a couple other raisin bran cereal brands, but your eyes keep going back to the first one. Why?

The Kellogg's Raisin Bran box made it easy for you. It answered the question of "Does this cereal meet my goals of eating less sugar and carbs?" by calling out "Less Sugar" and "10g Carbs" right on the box. They also remove an objective (tastes bad) by adding "Great Flavor" up front.

Resumé raisin bran is about turning your Resumé into a marketing tool for you. When you're in this game to win, think about calling attention to and focusing on the key points that employers need to know about you. In today's competitive, crowded market, standing out is essential to grabbing an employer's attention.

How do you stand out? Focus your Resumé on these seven areas:

1. Facts
2. Figures
3. Percentages
4. Specific accomplishes
5. Revenue
6. Numbers
7. Results

Having a Resumé that gets results is about marketing you in a way that employers see your best features *first*, just like the Kellogg's Raisin Bran box.

How do you polish up your current Resumé? Let's look at some real-life applications.

Real-Life Application: Resumés That Get Results

These examples are from people who've had their Resumés professionally reviewed and revised.

Objective and Summary Section: Reduced and Revised

Original Resumé Copy:

"Summary"

Results-driven Senior Manager with proven track record in generating and implementing successful brand marketing campaigns for reputable Marketing and Promotions Agency. Designs relevant initiatives to produce higher numbers in membership programs, grow event attendance, and increase company revenue. Strong communicator; builds long-term relationships by effectively managing brand marketer and entertainment executive expectations. Decisive and energetic; consistently demonstrates the ability to adapt to fast-paced environments. Capitalizes on excellent project management skills and follow through to achieve company and individual goals.

NEW, Powerful, Focused, Polished Resumé Copy:

"Management Summary"

Focused, motivated senior manager with 8+ years at industry-leading motion picture company Warner Bros; proven track record in generating and implementing successful branded marketing campaigns with Top 10 marketing and promotions agency; skilled communicator who builds long-term relationships by effectively managing brand marketer and entertainment executive communications.

Job Description Bullet Points :: Powerful and Polished

Original Resumé Copy:

- Increased departmental efficiency with training

NEW, Powerful, Focused and Polished Resumé Copy:

- Increased departmental efficiency by 30% through effective training and managing 12 promotional consultants and interns

Original Resumé Copy :

- Facilitated high-paced, bicoastal travel plans and meetings for EVP

NEW, Powerful, Focused and Polished Resumé Copy:

- Managed bicoastal travel schedule for 2 EVPs, facilitating 20+ trips annually year over year for 3 consecutive years

Original Resumé Copy

- Managed $700,000 marketing budget

NEW, Powerful, Focused and Polished Resumé Copy:

- Responsible for marketing budget of nearly $750,000 and managing national team of 6

As shown by the examples above, the key to bullet points, summary sections and all areas of your Resumé is answering one of two questions:

1. What did you do?
2. How did you do it?

Chapter 1.3 | Layout Counts: 1, 2, 3

Functional or chronological? One page or two pages? Do I need a summary section? If I had a dime for every time I was asked a question about Resumé layouts, I'd have…a lot of dimes.

The reality is this: layout counts, and I'm going to make it as easy as 1, 2, 3.

1. **KISS.**
   *K*eep it *S*traightforward and *S*imple: employers will love your Resumé so much they'll want to KISS you when you do this for them.

2. **Two Pages**
   This is the standard for 85% of professionals.

3. **Results Up Front and Center**
   Nearly 80% of hiring managers only read the top half of page one of your Resumé.

Basics only get you so far. Here's where I give you insider secrets to what the basics above *really* mean.

KISS: Keep it Straightforward and Simple

Resumés can easily become wordy and filled with every accomplishment and professional result in the past 15 years of your career. You might need to check your ego at the door to win the job search game.

Simplicity suggestions:

- Pull out highlighted contributions to place in the top half of your Resumé
- Keep positions that are only within the past 10-12 years
- Eliminate positions that are irrelevant to your current or future profession and industry
- Three to five bullets per position
- Select only key accomplishments for bullet points in each position

Can you recall ever seeing a friend's Resumé that had an objective at the top followed by a paragraph of text under each job title? How likely are you to read those paragraphs?

Now, imagine showing friends your new Resumé with selected contributions at the top, a polished summary, and focused, powerful bullet points for each position with numbers, facts and figures. You'll feel confident, and as soon as you see their response you'll love the way you feel.

Two Pages, 85% of the time

How do you know if you fall in the 85% or the other 15%?

The length of your Resumé depends on your length of service. Follow this simple guide to determine how many pages yours should be:

- Under 5 years: 1 page
- 5-10 years: 1-2 pages

- 10+ years: 2 pages

Outside of particular professional requirements (e.g., military officers, doctoral dissertations), never, ever submit a Resumé that is longer than two pages.

> **Real Life Testimonial**
>
> *"I received a Resumé for a senior sales executive that was 15 pages long. Why anyone, particularly in sales, would have a Resumé this long is beyond me. To top it off, he had his picture on it. It wasn't flattering. He was promptly put in File 13."* —senior recruiter

In the career and job industry, "File 13" is a term used for, well, the garbage. Stick to a Resumé length of two pages or less and you'll never again wonder if it is the right length.

Results: Up Front and Center

Why do nearly 80% of hiring managers only read the first half of your Resumé? It's the same reason that you watch the trailer before going to a movie or read the headline of a news article. If you want more information, you can find it later and so can the hiring manager. **When you put your best results up front on your Resumé, in the top half of page one, you draw the hiring manager in to look further. You achieve your desired result: landing the interview.**

Let's take a look at the before-and-after of a real-life Resumé focused on layout and getting results. It's important to know that hiring managers like fresh Resumés better than templates, so add your own personal touch.

Jenn**Foster**

312.424.7864 (cellular)   **jfoster@aggeus.com**

Accomplished executive with experience in implementing results-driven sales and marketing strategies in diverse markets, with limited and large budgets, on international and domestic soils.

Aggeus Healthcare, Chicago, IL   **2002 – Present**
Vice President, Operations

One of eight executive team members serving the needs of an organization noted as a Top 10 employer for more than 500 individuals.

- Responsible for the strategic development, implementation, and dissemination of marketing tactics for four senior living residences in Illinois and Tucson, three cafes, and more than 11 educational products and services
- Accompanied the CEO in successfully leading a 21-month communication effort between Mather LifeWays and Evanston City Council to gain approval to rebuild two existing buildings into a state-of-the-art retirement community
  - Obtained 231, $1,000 deposits, from interested consumers, prior to formal marketing efforts or hiring of salespeople
  - Exceeded pre-sales goals for $250 million-dollar senior living residence
- Direct management of ten staff members and several external agencies
- Part of a multi-disciplined team integrating sales, marketing, and operations exhibiting a strong ability to suture differing agendas and developing skill sets to achieve required business goals
- Initiated complete brand identify conversion, including logo design, tagline development, and style standard guidelines for a this 50+ year-old organization creating a unified portfolio among diverse locations and employee groups
- Serve as a liaison between facilities and management with [marketing] budget oversight for our senior living residences, café locations, and Institute on Aging
- Organizational spokesperson, along with the President and CEO

Sysco Foods, Chicago   **2002 – 2003 & 1997 – 1999**
Vice President, Account Services

Recruited to obtain new business and lead marketing efforts on behalf of existing client base. Managed agency's largest client, exceeding $13 million in annual sales; reported to President.

- Managed brand equity and budgets of major food brands, including Healthy Choice®, Butterball®, Reddiwip® and Egg Beaters®
- Formulated a landmark training program, materials, and incentive process for a team of 60 sales people, targeting restaurant operators across the country
- Generated a brand-awareness score of 99% based on developing a new product launch process
- Conducted quarterly workshops for clients, to ensure employees are well-informed of industry trends and implications (group size ranged from 10 to 200)
- Orchestrated classical marketing efforts including, direct mail, public relations, advertising, sales collateral, CD Rom Training, Website presence, trade shows, presentation templates and content, new product launches, and overall marketing and business plans

The Metropolitan Club Group,
United Kingdom and Scotland   **2001 – 2002**

International Director of Sales and Marketing
Recruited to manage the marketing and sales efforts of a private members club in the Highlands of Scotland and a boutique hotel in London, England. Relocated to the United Kingdom and Scotland; reported to Chairman of the Board.

- Increased stagnate U.S. business by 23% within eight months
- Fearlessly pursued new market segments to grow business in areas not previously tapped
- Lived on-site with responsibility, along with general manager, for day-to-day operations
- Initiated a 12-month strategic sales and marketing plan funded by the Chairman of the Board
- Tapped for numerous special projects including identifying value creation opportunities and conducting market due diligence
- Built strategic partnerships to create reciprocal opportunities among Clubs both domestically and internationally

The Park Hyatt, Chicago
Assistant Vice President

1999 — 2001

Managed the marketing and advertising efforts of Classic Residence by Hyatt, a nationally recognized leader in senior living; reported to COO.
- Managed 15-person team with marketing oversight for 22 properties across the country
- Stabilized department [employee] turnover by 100% during my tenure
- Saved an average of 30%, by implementing a vendor review policy to ensure competitive pricing on all outside purchases

BeLux Agency, Wisconsin
New Business and Account Director

1993 — 1997

Was hired as agencies first account executive and one of only eight employees in 1993—there were 45 employees when I exited the company in 1997, reported to President.

- Acquired one of the first accounts through cold-calling, which blossomed into $3 million dollars in billings
- Managed 45% of total agency billings, traveled extensively
- Quadrupled sales in a 24-month period via new business pitches with the president of the agency. Acquired Hershey's Foods, Marriott Educational Services, and Otis Spunkmeyer
- President of agency offered partnership opportunity and full payment of MBA during my tenure

Higher Education

❑ University of Chicago MBA – Completed program while working full-time, graduated 2008. Attended classes in North America, Singapore, and London.
❑ University of Wisconsin Oshkosh, Bachelor of Arts, Marketing Communication, Health Education, and Speech Communication
❑ Life experience; stepparent of one Girl Scout and one Brownie

Accomplishments

❑ 2007 and 2008 Mature Media Awards recognizing innovative marketing approaches
❑ 2007 and 2008 Innovation award from the National Association of Home Builders (NAHB), for marketing collateral development and design
❑ Achieved a top two placement in the 2007 International Business Plan Competition at the University of Chicago Graduate School of Business
❑ Active Board Member of Esperanza Community Services in Chicago, IL

AFTER:

Jenn**Foster**, MBA

312.424.7864   31 East Elm Street #3E, Chicago, IL 60610
jennfoster09@gmail.com

EXECUTIVE SUMMARY

Award-Winning Senior Executive brings 15+ years of operational excellence, savvy team leadership of 80 employees and budget management up to $200 Million. Global operational brand executive for Healthy Choice®, Butterball®, ReddiWip® and EggBeaters® ready to take on your challenge and make it a success.

Key Executive | Led 80 person regional team with $200+ million budget

Operational Guru | Reduced operational expenses 30% by implementing a vendor review and bidding process

Revenue Focused | Increased stagnate U.S. business 23% in 8 months by fearlessly pursuing new market segments

PROFESSIONAL EXPERIENCE

AGGEUS HEALTHCARE
CHICAGO, IL   2002 – PRESENT
VICE PRESIDENT, OPERATIONS

- Lead an 80 person regional team and oversee a $200+ million budget
- Responsible for strategic marketing for 4 senior living residences, 3 cafes and 11+ educational products servicing over 45,000 residents
- Successfully led a 21-month joint effort with local City Council to rebuild a state-of-the-art community
- Operational black belt suturing differing agendas together to achieve required business goals
- Initiated complete brand identity conversion for this 50+-year-old organization creating a unified portfolio
- Serve as organization's key spokesperson and operational liaison both internally and with the media

SYSCO FOODS
CHICAGO, IL   2002 – 2003
VICE PRESIDENT, ACCOUNT SERVICES   1997 – 1999

- Managed operational brand equity of major food brands, including Healthy Choice®, Butterball®, Reddiwip® and Egg Beaters®
- Formulated a landmark training program, materials, and incentive process for 60 + sales people
- Generated a brand-awareness score of 99% by developing an innovative product launch process
- Conducted quarterly workshops for over 1500 client participants on industry trends and implications

THE METROPOLITAN CLUB GROUP
UNITED KINGDOM AND FRANCE   2001 – 2002
INTERNATIONAL DIRECTOR OF SALES AND MARKETING

- Increased stagnate U.S. business 23% in first 8 months by fearlessly pursuing new market segments
- Lived on-site in United Kingdom with responsibility for $250K budget and day-to-day Club operations
- Built global strategic partnerships to develop reciprocal membership benefits among Clubs worldwide

THE HYATT GROUP
CHICAGO, IL   1999 — 2001
ASSISTANT VICE PRESIDENT

- Managed a 15-person team with marketing oversight for 22 properties
- Stabilized department and employee turnover by 108% during my tenure through cultural changes
- Reduced operational expenses 30% by implementing a vendor review and bidding process

EDUCATION & TRAINING

- ❑ **MBA** – University of Chicago, Booth School of Business Attended classes in North America, Singapore, and London
- ❑ **Bachelor of Arts** – University of Wisconsin, Oshkosh
  Major: Marketing Communication
- ❑ **Bachelor of Arts** - University of Wisconsin, Oshkosh
  Major: Health Education Minor: Speech Communication
- ❑ **The Leadership Advantage** - Dale Carnegie Training, Chicago, IL
- ❑ **The People Side of Process Improvement** - Dale Carnegie Training, Chicago, IL

AWARDS & COMMUNITY INVOLVEMENT

- ❑ Recipient (twice), Mature Media Awards, 2008 and 2007, recognizing innovative marketing approaches
- ❑ Recipient (twice) , Innovation award, 2008 and 2007
- ❑ Member, Board of Directors, Esperanza Community Services (2008-Present)

REFERENCES GLADLY FURNISHED UPON REQUEST

Chapter 1.4 | Top 10 Résumé Faux Pas

Even the best-designed, organized and cohesive résumé can reveal a faux pas. How do you make sure you don't make a mistake? That's what I'm here to help you with; to focus on the top 10 errors that recruiters and hiring managers see most often and notice more than others, so you can avoid them and make sure your résumé gets results. These résumé faux pas are nothing new and each of them has an easy fix, which I've provided. These basic changes and easy fixes are the difference between your résumé getting your desired result (the interview) and landing in the garbage—really. Whatever you do during your job search, make sure you avoid making these 10 résumé faux pas:

1. Spelling and Grammar Errors

Ladies and gentleman, I give you...drum roll, please...spell-check, which is step one. Step two is the power of the human eye. Spell-check only catches spelling errors, which means if you meant to say "lead" rather than "led," it won't catch it! I strongly recommend having a friend or a professional copyeditor look over your résumé for spelling and grammar issues, since you'll likely see only what you *think* you wrote versus what's actually there. (Take it from a gal who wrote a book. I swear my editor added in some spelling and grammar errors...)

a. It's and Its

Fix this faux pas by ensuring your résumé is free of glaring errors (this applies to your cover letters and e-mails to hiring managers, too). According to concisecorrect.com, the following are the most common typos seen in business communications today.

It's is short for "it is" or "it has." *It* is about possession.

Correct: It's in my range of capabilities to make the phone ring.
Correct: It's been a great year for e-commerce Websites.
Correct: This company and its standards are known throughout Chicago.

b. There, They're and Their

They're is short for "they are." Use *there* when referring to a place or to indicate the existence of something. *Their* is about possession.

Correct: They're the ones you want to impress.
Correct: There is a time and a place for polka dots.
Correct: If Maui is the place to be, I want to go there!
Correct: They love their Mac computers, right?

c. i.e. and e.g.

Both i.e. and e.g. have commas after them when used and usually a semicolon (;) before them. Both have distinct meanings. The term *i.e.* means "id est" in Latin or "that is [to say]" in English. The term *e.g.* means "exempli gratia" in Latin or "for example [*e*xample(s) *g*iven]" in English.

Correct: I oversee Doonelap's marketing team; i.e., Margaret Jones, Elisa Cohen, Amy Rhodes and Calvin Garcia

Correct: I oversee Doonelap's marketing efforts; e.g., Right Now direct mail campaign, Yale University campus presentations, Let's Go! Website launch

d. Effect and Affect

Effect is something brought about by a cause; *affect* means to have an influence on or to create a change in something.

Correct: Your attitude will affect your supervisor's opinion of you.

Correct: The effect of the music was obvious.

e. You're and Your

You're is short for "you are." *Your* is about possession.

Correct: You're a team player.

Correct: Your ability to multitask is really impressive.

f. Supposed (not *suppose*)

Supposed means something was planned to happen; *suppose* is a verb that's similar to "think" or "assume."

Correct: I suppose we could start the meeting at noon.

Correct: We were supposed to go to St. Louis instead of Dallas.

g. Than (not *then*)

Than is about comparing. *Then* is used as a time marker that means "after," "afterward," "next," or "later."

Correct: We ordered the supplies and then we drank the coffee.

Correct: That meeting ended sooner than expected.

h. Try to (not *try and*)

Try and separates two activities while *try to* links them. In the example below, if you wrote *try and rework*, you're trying *and* reworking rather than just reworking.)

Correct: I will try to rework the agenda so your presentation is included.

i. That and Which

This is the #1 typo seen in business communications (and in personal, everyday use). *That* has to do with essential information related to the intended meaning of the sentence. *That* is not offset by commas. *Which* is used when including information that otherwise would not be provided. *Which* is offset by commas.

Correct: The delivery that arrived yesterday was correct.

Correct: The delivery, which arrived yesterday, was correct.

Correct: Angela's speech, which I'll repeat in a few minutes, was amazing.

Correct: I'm about to cook dinner, which is something I don't do very often.

Correct: This is something that needs to be addressed.

2. Storytelling

I love telling, reading and hearing stories, and you might also. Your résumé is not the place for any kind of storytelling, though. You don't need any extra words.

Fix this faux pas by remembering to KISS your prospective employer: Keep it *S*traightforward and *S*imple.

3. Pictures

Nix the pics. No bikini shots (yes, it's been seen). No group photos (another true story). Do not put a photo of your leg and a high heel shoe with "this will get me in the door" on the cover of your résumé (she was applying for a sales *executive* job!).

Fix this faux pas by saving fun pictures for your friends and family.

4. Crazy Contact Information

yoohoo@yahoo.com
runnerdude@gmail.com
adkz38@aol.com
katenkids@msn.com

Cute, fun, unique, crazy e-mail addresses are just that...what they are not is professional.

Fix this faux pas by creating a standard, professional e-mail address for your résumé and job search (e.g., katepetersen@gmail.com).

5. Defunct Details

You have the hiring manager or recruiter's attention. He/She likes you. Recruiter Jan picks up the phone, dials your number and hears, "I'm sorry. You've reached a number that is no longer in service." Or "The Verizon Wireless subscriber you're trying to reach is no longer active."

Oh, yes, this happens far more often than you think it does. Why? Because people update their employment information and forget to update the contact information.

Can it get worse? Sure it can. It's offer time and the only thing left is to check your references. Hiring manager Ken looks at your résumé, sends off an e-mail to three of your references and gets back the dreaded MAILER-DAEMON: "Message Undeliverable: Your message delivery failed because the recipient no longer has a mailbox on this server."

Ken really likes you, so he thinks; I'll try to call Reference X...only he hears the same recording that Recruiter Jan got earlier that day from a different candidate. Now Ken thinks to himself, if this guy can't keep track of his three employment references, how is he going to keep track of our customers or reports? Maybe I should call our #2 candidate in for another interview.

Fix this faux pas by ensuring your contact information is up to date. Also, make sure your e-mail inbox, cell phone voice mail box and home answering machine are not "full" to capacity, which would bounce new messages.

6. Irrelevant Information

Did you work your way through college? I did—I started working at age 11 in a pizza parlor answering phones (thanks, Josh). It's not the kind of thing I put on my résumé, though. You would be surprised by how many people do.

Fix this faux pas by only including positions that are relevant and excluding anything irrelevant to your industry, profession and professional career within the past 10-12 years.

7. Too Personal

If you coach your son's little league team or volunteer at your daughter's Girl Scout meetings, leave it off your resumé. The same goes for your commitment to your church council board and weekly homeless shelter volunteering.

This is often confused in the "community involvement" section of a resumé. Focus on boards of directors you sit on and organizations that you chair that are unaffiliated with protected classes such as race, religion, national origin, age and sexual orientation. Employers can use this information to discriminate against you based on age, parental status, marital status and even religion. (Something safe would be the American Alliance for Theatre and Education.)

Fix this faux pas by omitting personal information on your resumé.

8. References Omitted

Employers want to know that you're unafraid to be checked out when and if they choose to do so.

Fix this faux pas by including "References Gladly Furnished Upon Request" at the bottom of your resumé.

> **Insider Tip:** A recent survey by the Society of Human Resources Management reported that 89% of human resources (HR) managers conduct reference checks.

9. You are Spam

Did you know that sending your résumé as a Microsoft Word (.doc) attachment may mean your résumé will not be opened? Employers have become more concerned about viruses and have increased their anti-spam software, which means your attachment may automatically put you in the spam folder.

Fix this faux pas by e-mailing your résumé as a PDF attachment. (Never copy and paste your résumé into an e-mail!)

10. Conversion Confusion

Job boards are notorious for requesting a .txt (text only) or scanable version of your résumé. You'll be surprised at the confused and sad state in which your résumé appears when it arrives on the recruiter's desk if you upload a (.doc) file or simply convert your Word file to a (.txt) file and submit it.

Fix this faux pas by checking out the <u>Do-It-Yourself Résumé Kit</u> at <u>www.adrianallames.com</u>, which provides a professional example of a nicely prepared, clean résumé in a text-only, scanable format.

Now that your résumé is in great shape, let's look at its teammate in paper, if you will: your cover letter.

Chapter 1.5 | Catchy Cover Letters

"Good is the enemy of great."
—Jim Collins, Author of *Good to Great*

Your résumé is organized, laid out well and you've made sure it has no faux pas. It feels good knowing your professional life just had a makeover, and you want to blast it out to the universe.

Hold off on hitting that send button for just a few more minutes. Right about now your résumé is great but, as a candidate, you appear good and you deserve to appear as you are: great. To show an employer just how great you are is going to take highlighting it for them in a catchy cover letter.

Buzz terms like "results-oriented," "on time" and "under budget" or "client-focused" will quickly lose the employer's attention. Catchy cover letters are personalized, focused and brief.

Catchy cover letters feature three things:
1. The employer's needs
2. The employer's bottom line
3. What you can do to meet and improve #1 and #2

Your résumé is all about you. The cover letter is all about the employer.

———

Dear employer,

You are amazing. You're the most wonderful employer in the city and anyone would be lucky to work for you. Please interview me.

Sincerely,
Your future employee of the month

———

Okay, not quite the kind of cover letter you want to write, but you get the point. Focus on the company's needs and how you and your skills meet their needs better than any other candidate. Let's take a look at a catchy cover letter and how it can transform you from a good package to a great package:

MICHAEL GRAY

454 Wetherbee Rd. • Orlando, Florida 32824• (407) 555-1842 •
mkgray@gmail.com

May 2, 2010

FedEx Corporate
Attn: Michelle Goettler
9520 Central Florida Pkwy
Orlando, FL 32824

RE: Marketing Director, #K36501

Dear Ms. Goettler,

FedEx's Fortune 100 Best Companies to Work for in 2010 rating captured my attention and inspires me to contribute my talents in the role of **Marketing Director.** My expertise creating global marketing plans for Fortune 100 Kraft and their leading brand DiGiornio, will allow me to hit the ground running.

In that role, I managed advertising relationships with Top 10 Media Agency Starcom MediaVest leading promotional agency Ryan Partnership as well as a team of 15 marketing professionals.

FedEx will benefit from 10+ years of marketing expertise and successes including:

- Building marketing strategies that lead to success from both a client and revenue perspective
- Managing budgets of up to $20 Million and teams of more than 10+ employees
- Creating F100 CPG marketing plans that increased brand revenue over 25% YOY

Congratulations on your Best Companies to Work for in 2010 award and I look forward to discussing the Marketing Director opportunity. Please contact me at (312) 555-1842 to schedule a time for us to meet in person.

Sincerely,
(Insert scanned signature here)
Michael Gray

Why does Michael's cover letter work? Seven areas stand out. Here are the things he did right:

1. Properly format your letter.
   a. Using standard business letter format is important.
   b. Convey knowledge of grammar and written communication skills to the employer.
   c. Allow the hiring manager to easily read the letter.

2. Clearly identify the job title and job requisition number up front.
   a. If a hiring manager or recruiter has a hard time locating this, it'll be tossed.
   b. Ensures your résumé and cover letter are routed to the correct hiring manager.
   c. Many résumés and cover letters are received by entry-level recruiters, assistants or executive assistants. This information helps sort them.

3. Focus on the company.
   a. Two paragraphs start with the company name.
   b. One paragraph starts by congratulating the company.
   c. The letter doesn't start with "I" or "me."

4. Strongly connect employer, position and your results.
   a. Top two paragraphs have direct results.
   b. Middle three bullet points highlight employer needs for this position.

5. Show confidence.
   a. Don't hold back your accomplishments.

6. Make a call to action.
    a. Your last sentence must include at least a phone number.

7. Include your updated contact information.
    a. Place how to reach you up front.
    b. Place how to reach you in the call to action.
    c. Place how to reach you in your signature.

How can you write a similar cover letter that will be just as focused and catchy? Use the same format Michael did or change it up to suit your personality. Find a unique statistic about the company using Google; include it right up front to make a fast, personal connection with the reader. Then, flow right into the position and directly connect your accomplishments and expertise. Next, integrate figures, facts and results from your résumé, keeping the wording focused on the company. Ask yourself, "How does this result, accomplishment or skill *benefit the company?*"

When you have the answer, word it into a powerful statement. Let the confidence burst out of you until you have your own catchy cover letter.

Last, always end with a call to action. Forget the "I look forward to hearing from you"; let everyone else in the job search game look forward to hearing from them. Ask them outright to call you and set up a meeting.

Now, grab your catchy new cover letter and put it right next to your résumé. Suffice it to say, you have yourself a great team working on your behalf.

Chapter One | Résumés That Get Results | Review

Chapter 1.1 | It's All About You
- The #1 goal of your résumé is to land an interview
- Focus on facts, figures, results and accomplishments
- This is your time to shine and brag about you, you, you

Chapter 1.2 | Résumé Raisin Bran
- Your résumé is product marketing
- Call out key accomplishments and address objectives
- Answer questions for employers before they ask them
  - o Less Sugar, Less Carbs, Great Flavor
  - o Budget management to $5M, teams of 10+, self-motivated

Chapter 1.3 | Layout Counts: 1, 2, 3
- Nearly 80% of hiring managers only read the top half of your résumé
- Focus on key contributions
- KISS prospective employers and keep your résumé to two pages

Chapter 1.4 | Top 10 Résumé Faux Pas
- 1-3: Spelling errors, storytelling and pictures
- 4-6: Crazy contact information, defunct details and irrelevant information
- 7-9: Too personal, references omitted and you are spam
- 10: Conversion confusion

Chapter 1.5 | Catchy Cover Letters

- Properly format your letter
- Clearly identify the job title and job requisition number up front
- Focus on the company
- Strongly connect employer, position and your results
- Show confidence
- Make a call to action
- Include your updated contact information

Résumés are two pages of your life's work, and for more than a decade, I've coached people on how to creatively describe their personality, professional accomplishments and expertise in less than two pages. It's not easy to create a résumé that gets results and rocks; if it was easy, everyone would have one! Take your time and do as many drafts as it takes. This is a representation of you, and you need it to be just right.

You now have the tools, information and resources to develop a powerful, polished résumé (and cover letter!) that gets results—the first way to win the job search game. Let's move on to creating your own personal brand.

CHAPTER TWO

PERSONAL BRANDING

	9		6			3		
				8	3			5
2					7			
	8					5		
3							4	
	1							2
		7						
1			5		9		6	
		4		3		7		

"Being CEO of Me Inc. requires you to act selfishly—to grow yourself, to promote yourself, to get the market to reward yourself."

-Tom Peters

Nike's swoosh logo is identifiable around the world. The golden arches of McDonalds are known by kids as young as two in more than 100 countries around the globe. Mention the word Starbucks and people immediately think of coffee. Budweiser brings to mind good ol' American beer. The Four Seasons brand evokes first-class service and luxury accommodations.

Branding is all about who you are, what image you want people to have of you and what reputation you want left behind when you are gone.

Starting now, think of yourself differently. As of today, you're a brand. You're not an "employee" at Ford, a "manager" at Discover Financial Services, a "team member" at United Airlines, a "human resource" at Procter & Gamble or anywhere else for that matter. YOU are a brand—not defined by a job title, company, position or job description.

Chapter 2.1 | YOU as Brand Manager

You're every bit as much of a brand as Amazon, Marriott, Olive Garden, 1-800-Flowers and Gatorade.

What do the brands you love most convey to you and how? Think of brands like Coca-Cola, Subway, Victoria's Secret or Adidas and the brand managers responsible for creating the way you feel, respond to and purchase based on their brands. Brand managers have to ask themselves: What is it that makes my product different? What is my product's *unique value proposition* or *UVP*?

I recently purchased laundry detergent, something I regret to admit I do far too infrequently. As I looked at the overwhelming choices in the aisle at Target (another great brand), I narrowed it down to Cheer or Purex—primarily because my mom has both in her laundry room.

Purex, in a nondescript yellow bottle, had this great new 3-in-1 cleaning angle (super-concentrated, softener and anti-static) and being the bottom-line, get-it-done kind of gal I am, I thought it looked pretty good to me. Plus, it was on sale and I love a sale. Cheer was in a bright blue bottle and focused on being "color safe" and "naturally free and clear." Sale or safety of my clothes?

Cheer won. Why? Branding. The Cheer brand manager communicated 100% of what I needed. My white and colored clothes would be safe from my tragic laundry skills.

Plus, I can rest easy knowing I will not break out in hives during a "9 Ways to Win the Job Search" Boot Camp from some unnatural dye.

The first point about personal branding is that your brand message needs to grab the attention of a potential employer. One of the ways this works is to use the feature-to-benefit model. Every feature offered by a product or service is immediately followed by an identifiable benefit. This worked in the Cheer example. Another brand that uses the feature-to-benefit model well is Nordstrom department stores. The primary feature is Nordstrom's personal service provided to each and every customer. The identifiable customer benefit is the *feeling of individual attention.*

Let's expand on the brand message and feature-to-benefit concepts by delving into your unique value proposition or UVP.

Chapter 2.2 | Your Unique Value Proposition

In today's competitive market, the most successful job seekers are those who understand the value of marketing and apply it to themselves. They use the same tactics that successful brands have used for decades.

It's time to focus on your unique value proposition or UVP.

A Unique Value Proposition (UVP) is any aspect of an object that differentiates it from similar objects. (Wikipedia.org)

Examples of leading UVPs:

- Head & Shoulders: "You get rid of dandruff"
- Domino's Pizza: "You get fresh, hot pizza delivered to your door in 30 minutes or less—or it's free."
- FedEx: "When your package absolutely, positively has to get there overnight."
- M&Ms: "Melts in your mouth, not in your hand."

Before Head & Shoulders created its famous "You get rid of dandruff," the brand team likely spent hours and hours, if not days and months, deciding the *specific benefit* they wanted customers to focus on. If Karl has dandruff, he probably wants to get rid of it. It looks like a *solution* to Karl's *problem* that exists.

When it comes to YOU as a brand, the same concept applies. The UVP of YOU is about what differentiates you from other job seekers in a similar profession and industry. Finding the right direction for your job search will lead to a focused UVP. Following are five questions for you to answer:

1. Where have I been in my career?
2. Where do I want to go with my career?
3. How do I want to get to where I want to go?
4. What are my three key professional accomplishments?
5. What skills do I have that are "industry agnostic"?

YOU are a brand now. When creating the UVP of YOU, it's important to carefully examine the qualities, abilities and skills that make you different from other brands (aka other people vying for the same job):

- Characteristics
- Features
- Skills
- Work experience
- Leadership experience
- Education and training
- Professional memberships (particularly boards of directors)

What is the *one* thing that makes you unique in comparison to any other candidate applying for the same job? What makes you the most attractive candidate? How can you make yourself more attractive? The way you define yourself is what creates your UVP and competitive advantage.

- Identify competitive advantages to build a UVP.
- Carefully select competitive advantages—different employers want different skills.

Given the amount of professionals who have to shift industries in today's difficult economic climate, I recommend sourcing your work and leadership experience for skills that transfer between industries. These are called "industry agnostic" skills. Following are a few to get you started:

- Managing people: supervisor, team leader, manager, director, vice president, etc.
- Budget management: P&L, budgets
- Client relations
- Customer service
- Accounting
- Report creation and management
- Account management
- Travel planning or organization
- Event planning
- Territory management
- Cold calling
- Strategic marketing plan development
- Database management

- Client relationship management
- Presentation to C-level executives
- Innovative campaign designs
- Graphic design: brochures, logos
- Website design

Here are some parameters for developing your UVP that will help you determine when to use it in comparison to your powerful 30-second pitch, which you'll be developing later. Keep your UVP to 15 words or less and be able to say it in less than 15 seconds. This is called the 15/15 rule. If you need to make a stellar impression or you're very shy and want to prompt the other person to ask questions, your UVP is your go-to statement to make the right impression in less than 15 seconds and less than 15 words.

"Award-winning graphic designer for ten years"
-Conveys experience, talent and that this person is a graphic designer; seven words

"Chief Finance Executive for seven years at Fortune 500 companies specializing in turnaround scenarios"
-Conveys C-level company size and area of expertise; 14 words

"National Salesman of the Year. Brought in $3 Million; 20% more than any other sales director"
-Award-winning salesman, carries and exceeds multimillion dollar quotas; 14 words

None of these UVPs are industry focused and yet they all convey competitive advantages as well as enough details about what the person does to tell a potential employer where he or she can fit into the organization.

Imagine you're an employer who needs fresh marketing materials, has been thinking about adding a CFO to your senior management team or beefing up your sales staff. Is there any reason why you wouldn't ask for these people's information? You'd follow-up for a meeting based on these concise, clean and focused UVPs.

Chapter 2.3 | The Powerful 30-Second Pitch

One of the most common questions asked in our society when we first meet someone is "What do you do?" Get ready to fire up your quick-'n-dirty "elevator" speech. How did this get its name? The average time a person spends in an elevator is about 15 seconds. You should be able to summarize who you are and your goals in that time frame should you ever find yourself with a captive audience—aka someone who's hiring—on an elevator (yes, it happens more often than you think).

If you're currently job searching, answering the "What do you do?" question quickly becomes an uncomfortable situation and one that you're likely facing every day if not multiples times a day. Now that you have your new UVP, you can answer that question confidently—in less than 15 words and 15 seconds.

If you're at a networking event, coffee shop, a Fourth of July gathering or anywhere you want to or are required to supply a response, simply deliver your skillfully crafted UVP. Pow! Fifteen seconds later, you are given prompt attention. Most of the time, you will then be asked a question. This is where your powerful 30-second pitch comes into play.

The follow-up to your UVP is your powerful 30-second pitch. This pitch is a more elaborate, defined and detailed version of who you are and why you should be hired. Once your powerful 30-second pitch is complete, you'll walk into any situation thinking, Hello, world. I have, hands down, *the* most confident way to answer the "What do you do?" question. "Tell you about myself?" Sure! I'm about to say an impressive and commanding statement that will knock your socks off and put me at the top of your list.

The best part of your answer is that people will be impressed, and you'll likely have someone follow up with, "Tell me more…" or "We should talk…" Well, of course you should talk—he or she has just met the most interesting person of the evening: YOU. How many other people are going to respond as great as you just did? The rest of the night, people are droning "I'm a brand manager for Jell-O at Kraft Foods" or "I'm a creative director at Draft FCB" or "I'm blah, blah, blah." Snooze.

If you're thinking to yourself that you don't have such a pitch, you can relax. That's where I come in. The next two pages are step-by-step exercises that give you what you need to create your powerful 30-second pitch. Let's go.

Step 1:

Who Are You and What Do You Do?

If you use any personal information in your powerful 30-second pitch—this is where it goes—you want to keep it to a minimum. *Always remember to use your name.*

Example: "I'm Kim (Anders), a senior marketing and sales executive in the online media industry."

Step 2:

Your Accomplishments and What They Bring to the Table

Talk about your experiences and accomplishments and focus on facts and figures. If you're in front of a prospective employer, tailor your accomplishments to how they will *benefit* that employer and satisfy his or her needs.

Example: "Most recently at 360 Media, I was responsible for a global team of 25 and $75M in sales, showing year over year growth of 125% on average in the three years I was there.
Prior to that, I was the VP of sales at Focus Media, where I led a 10-person national sales team with a quota of $30M."

Step 3:

Why You Will Be/Are Successful

If in front of a potential employer, make the connection for him or her—*why* you will be successful at his or her company and how he or she can't live without you as part of the team. If at a networking event or literally in an elevator with someone, keep the theme general and focus on more generic themes.

Example: "I find the best part of being in sales is that my skills are transferable. I'm grateful that I was able to manage such talented salespeople and work for a successful company that allowed me to be a part of the senior management team and travel globally. Managing teams abroad, learning international customs, and implementing new systems, processes and procedures in places like Japan and London is an experience I'm looking forward to leveraging at a new company."

Putting It All Together: Complete Powerful 30-Second Pitch
Version 1:

"I'm Kim (Anders), a senior marketing and sales executive in the online media industry. Most recently at 360 Media as their senior VP of sales and marketing, I was responsible for $75M in sales, a global sales team of 25 and am proud to say that for the past three years, 360 Media showed 125% year over year growth. Expanding my management to Asia and the U.K., learning international customs, and implementing new systems, processes and procedures globally brought the company $10M in new revenue in 2009, and I'm looking forward to leveraging that experience in a new organization."

Version 2:

"I'm Kim, a senior marketing and sales executive in the online media industry. I've been with 360 Media, where I led a global sales team of 25 and increased the company's annual revenue by 125% year over year, resulting in $75M in sales. Just prior to that, I was with Focus Media as the VP of sales and marketing, where I led a national sales team of 10 and carried a $30M quota. I've really enjoyed the global expansion, team management and revenue growth in the past few years, which I'm excited to transfer to a new industry in the near future."

As "Project Runway" guru Tim Gunn says, "Make it work."

If there's one piece of advice I can share from my 10+ years of coaching clients, it's that there's only one way to make it work: *Practice. Practice. Practice.*

Chapter 2.4 | Personal Branding Dos and Don'ts

As with everything, there are definitely dos and don'ts when it comes to personal branding. Here are some guidelines to help you when crafting your personal brand:

- **Do** make your UVP and powerful 30-second pitch sound natural, conversational and effortless.
- **Do** focus on your competitive advantage.
- **Do** write, rewrite and focus your pitch to eliminate awkwardness.
- **Do** practice, practice and practice some more.
- **Do** avoid leaving the listener asking "So what?"
- **Do** consider a compelling "hook," prompting the listener to ask a question thus keeping the conversation going.
- **Don't** let your pitch or UVP sound canned.
- **Do** have a unique pitch that's exciting.
- **Do** incorporate your personality—make it fun.
- **Do** be warm, friendly and enthusiastic with your delivery.
- **Don't** rush your pitch—take it slow.
- **Do** maintain eye contact with your listener.
- **Don't** use jargon or acronyms that industry outsiders may not know.
- **Do** develop different versions of your pitch for different situations.
- **Do** wrap it up early if your listener's eyes glaze over or you lose his or her attention.

- **Do** use stories in your pitch—it makes your pitch more memorable.
- **Don't** be afraid to leave your UVP or powerful 30-second pitch as a voice mail.
- **Do** use your family, friends and pets as practice people.

When it comes to personal branding, YOU are the product you are delivering to another person. It's wise to consider the adage, "It's not what you say; it's how you say it." In this case, both *how and what* you say are equally important.

Chapter Two | Personal Branding | Review

Chapter 2.1 | You as Brand Manager

- You're a brand, just as Nike, Coca-cola and Olive Garden are brands.
- Implement the feature-to-benefit model.
- Create an attention-grabbing message of your brand.

Chapter 2.2 | Your Unique Value Proposition and Direction

- Create a UVP that's 15 words and said in 15 seconds.
- Identify the one thing that makes you unique.

Chapter 2.3 | Powerful 30-Second Pitch

- Use the three steps to design your pitch.
- Put it all together: three steps to 30-second pitch perfection.
- Make it work with practice, practice, practice.

Chapter 2.4 | Personal Branding Dos and Don'ts

When I started coaching 12 years ago, I never thought a job search book would have an entire chapter dedicated to the power of personal branding. Then again, I didn't think I would open today's *New York Times* to read that it had laid off 300 staff members and replaced two of the four "World News with Diane Sawyer" staff members with digital news producers.

Times have changed and it's affected the job search game in a big way. To win the game today, YOU have to be your own brand manager. YOU are a product.

The one thing I love about that is that you're *the* best possible brand manager you can hire to represent you. Who can position you better than you?

Now that you have the steps, tools and advice to create your UVP and powerful 30-second pitch, it's time to put it to use and move on to the third way to win the job search game: impressive interviews. Let's go.

Hiring managers watch out…recruiters beware…you'll be landing interviews and impressing employers in no time.

CHAPTER THREE

IMPRESSIVE INTERVIEWS

	9		6			3		
				8	3			5
2					7			
	8					5		
3				3			4	
	1							2
		7						
1			5		9		6	
		4		3		7		

"Many hiring managers make up their minds in the first eight seconds."

-Kate Stout, *Essortment*

What if you knew during an interview that the hiring manager was either rooting for or against you? Take a deep breath.

By the time you're done reading this chapter, you'll never again wonder if he or she is rooting for you—you'll know for sure that Rhonda or Joe or Bill is, in fact, rooting for you.

Chapter 3.1 | The First 8 Seconds and Preparing Effectively

Recently I had dinner with the CEO of a health care company that provides medical staff to 700 nursing homes in 14 states across the U.S. When I asked him if he decides in the first eight seconds if he's going to hire a new doctor, operations director or other staff member, his response surprised me. He said, "It's probably less than that. I decide almost immediately and find myself rooting for them or against them during the rest of the interview."

What can you do to ensure that the next hiring manager you interview with is rooting for you during the interview? Impress him or her during those first eight seconds using these first impression tips and tactics.

1. Arrive Promptly

Few things are worse than showing up late when it comes to first impressions. It's pretty hard to impress a hiring manager in the first eight seconds if you're not there yet! Give yourself plenty of time to find the office; I recommend twice the time that the directions say it'll take (e.g., MapQuest.com says it'll take you 45 minutes with traffic; leave 90 minutes before the interview to find the office).

Insider Tip: Earlier isn't always better. The ideal time to arrive, according to Emily Post's *The Etiquette Advantage in Business*, is 10 minutes before your scheduled meeting time. If you arrive too far in advance, the interviewer may feel rushed and/or you may appear desperate.

If you arrive 15+ minutes in advance, find a local coffee shop, grab a cup of joe, and review your notes and interview questions. You can relax your mind before the interview. Just keep an eye on your watch so you still make it back to the office and in the company's lobby 10 minutes before your interview time. **Remember to be polite and courteous to *everyone* you meet**; you never know if the CEO is the person walking in before you and holding the door or if the receptionist has a say in who's hired.

2. Appropriate Attire

People make judgments based on appearance all day long, and interviews are no exception. One of the most common questions I get is, "The recruiter said that everyone dresses casually and I should feel comfortable dressing the same. Is that okay to do?" My answer is always the same: "No."

In today's übercasual business world, deciding what to wear to an interview can be a real challenge. It's important to always look put-together, well groomed and like a seasoned professional. High-quality, tailored business suits are always appropriate for both men and women when interviewing. If it's a more casual environment, simply lose the tie or downplay your accessories.

You'll want to avoid dressing casual for an interview, even if you're meeting at a coffee shop. Never wear clothing that's too tight, revealing or sloppy.

"The devil is in the details"—this applies to interviewing too. Make sure your shoes are polished, especially in winter months. Ladies, ensure your nails are polished, but avoid loud or trendy colors. Make sure your hair is well groomed and that your hygiene is taken care of as well. You want the interviewer to see you before they smell you, so shower the morning of the interview using a clean-scent soap, and avoid using cologne or perfume that day, especially given the frequency of fragrance allergies these days.

Keep makeup and jewelry minimal and your tattoos covered.

3. Handshake

The power of a handshake is like no other description of a person. Really.

Shake with a medium-firm grip and you have immediately conveyed authority and poise. Give a limp hand and you're branded as meek and hesitant. If you're one of the bone-crushing shakers, you come off as overenthusiastic or domineering. All this from the few seconds of a handshake? That's right. Isabel the interviewer extends her hand and within a second or two, Isabel has a complete view of who you are.

How do you know what your handshake feels like? If you're a medium-firm grip kind of person, you've likely been complimented on the quality of your grip. A bone-crusher has seen the reaction on someone's face…oh, yes…you know it too, don't you? And if you're a limp hand shake, you know that too because you tend to have a gentleness about your entire personality.

When it comes to winning the job search game, the winning grip is medium-firm, and if you can switch your grip to a medium-firm grip, you'll convey confidence and authority in the first eight seconds. You will have the interviewer rooting for you the rest of the interview.

4. Body Language

A study conducted at the University of California, Los Angeles, found that 55% of communication is received from body language. This means you can say nothing and still have a 55% chance landing the job. (Okay, it doesn't mean that.) What it does mean is that it is just as important to pay attention to what you *do* in the interview as it is to what you say.

To convey confidence during the interview, use these body language tips:

- Sit up straight.
- Keep your shoulders back.
- Avoid crossing your legs (ladies, cross your ankles if you need to).
- Maintain eye contact.

Insider Tip: Duplicating interviewer body language makes them feel like you're "one of them" and belong at the company (e.g., if the interviewer leans forward, wait a minute and then lean forward). This works well; however, avoid imitating casual body poses.

Placing your hands in your pockets, over your mouth or under your legs conveys the message that you're either hiding something or lying. Avoid making these gestures.

Last, bad breath is a great way to ruin a first impression. Keep a tin of mints (never gum) handy in your car and pop one in just as you walk to the office. Finish the mint prior to your introduction.

When you arrive—10 minutes early, of course—walk in to the office and politely say to the receptionist:

"My name is Adriana Llames, and I'm here for a 2 p.m. interview with Ben Jameson."

If he or she offers you a glass of water or cup of coffee, politely decline. You want to avoid being uncomfortable from a full bladder in the middle of the interview.

Chapter 3.2 | 3 Ways to Answer the "Fit" Question

Every company has to determine if you're going to fit in with their culture and environment. This is referred to as the inevitable "fit" question: Is she going to fit here at Warner Bros.? Do you think he will fit with our team dynamic?

The insane thing to me about the whole fit thing is that you never know who's going to fit until they're a part of the team! When I owned my first company, 6 Degrees, I remember hiring this young woman who worked for a technology company. We got along great. I had her do some contract work for me and thought she would be a great employee. She seemed like the right fit for my growing company.

I was wrong. I was very wrong, and it was a costly mistake in more ways than one. Could I have known beforehand that it was going to be a blunder? No. She's a good person; she just wasn't a good fit for my company.

So, how do you answer the fit question for a hiring manager when he or she is interviewing you? Subconsciously. Over the years I've developed three distinct ways for you to overcome this objection, and I'm going to share them with you so you can impress the hiring manager and land the job.

1st Way to Answer the Fit Question ➡ Look the Part

People hire people who look like they belong at the company. How do you make yourself look like you fit?

Wear the company colors in your interview attire. Yes, it's that easy.

Following are some examples of how to make this work with actual companies and a real-life testimonial of a candidate who did just this to win the job search game and land a new job.

These images may be subject to copyright and trademarks. They're only used to represent colors and the association of them in interviewing practices.

Company: Mattel
             Kellogg's
             Coca-Cola
             Lego
             Burger King

Interview Attire: Integrate red: I recommend wearing a red scarf (ladies) or solid red tie (men). Avoid wearing a red suit as it's too overpowering.

Company: Kraft Foods
             Unilever
             P&G
             Intel
             PepsiCo
             Cadbury
             General Mils
             Philips
             AT&T
             Nokia
             IBM

Interview Attire: Integrate the matching blue color: I recommend wearing a blue blouse (ladies) or solid blue tie (men).

Real-Life Application

I had a career coaching client who was interviewing at Warner Bros. on a Thursday. When I asked what she was wearing she told me a gray suit with a white shirt and black shoes. Her outfit sounded perfectly appropriate and professional; however, I knew it could be kicked up a notch to overcome the fit objection and subconsciously answer the question, "Does she fit in here at Warner Bros.?"

My suggestion was that she buys a blue blouse to match the Warner Bros. blue and wear that instead of the white blouse. Keep the gray suit and black shoes. I explained the rationale and she agreed. She also integrated the next two ways (below) to address the fit question and she's starting at Warner Bros. a week from this coming Tuesday. *I* didn't get her the job, but wearing the Warner Bros. blue and impressing the interviewer certainly did help my client win the job search game.

2nd Way to Answer the Fit Question ➡ **Show Them You Belong**

Now that you look the part, let's show hiring managers you belong with a creative presentation that reinforces what you say. I developed this creative interview kit more than seven years ago, and my career coaching clients have been using it with great success ever since. When you use the kit, you accomplish four key interview goals:

- Show the company you fit in and belong there.
- Highlight four of your key skills and the job's requirements.
- Focus the interviewer's attention on YOU.
- Keep you top of mind after you leave the interview.

What is the creative interview kit and how does it look? It has four components and the best part is that it's easy to create a Word, PC or Mac version.

Page 1: Clear vinyl cover—provided by FedEx Office, etc.
Page 2: Creative cover letter—(Not to be confused with the letter you drafted in chapter one.)
Page 3: Your résumé—this is already done, thanks to chapter one.
Page 4: Black vinyl back cover—provided by FedEx Office, etc.

Put it all together, in the order above with a coil bind and you're ready to impress every hiring manager you meet. Let's show you what page two, the creative cover letter, looks like since it's what visually shows the interviewer that you belong.

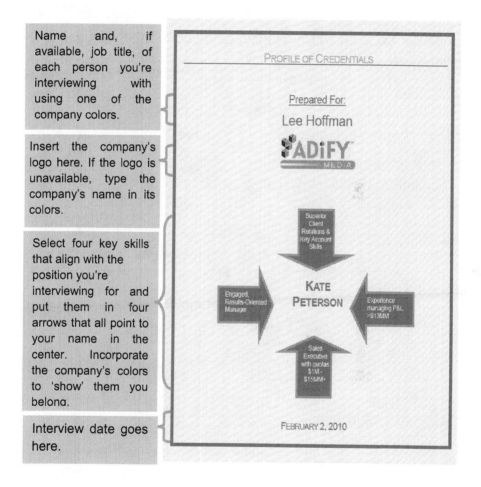

Name and, if available, job title, of each person you're interviewing with using one of the company colors.

Insert the company's logo here. If the logo is unavailable, type the company's name in its colors.

Select four key skills that align with the position you're interviewing for and put them in four arrows that all point to your name in the center. Incorporate the company's colors to 'show' them you belong.

Interview date goes here.

PROFILE OF CREDENTIALS

Prepared For:

Lee Hoffman

ADiFY
MEDIA

Superior
Client
Relations &
Key Account
Skills

Engaged,
Results-Oriented
Manager

KATE
PETERSON

Experience
managing P&L
>$13MM

Sales
Executive
with quotas
$1M -
$15MM+

FEBRUARY 2, 2010

In today's new job search game, more companies are conducting multiple interviews with each candidate. You may find yourself in a situation where you have two, three, four or even five interviews at the same company on the same day. When it comes to this situation, I recommend creating a customized creative cover letter for each interviewer.

There are also occasions when you have an interview and don't know the name of the interviewer. What do you do if you don't know who you'll be interviewing with? Create a creative interview kit customized to the company and leave the name/title section blank (e.g., part one of Figure 2.1).

Once you're done with the creative cover letter, it's time to put it all together.

Find a local printer. I personally love the printing online feature from FedEx Office at www.fedexoffice.com (I don't get any royalties from them, although now I'm thinking it might not be a bad idea if they gave everyone who read this book a discount. I'll work on that…). All you do is upload the creative cover letter (.doc) file, followed by your résumé (.doc) file, and then select your print options. The print option is when you select coil bind with a clear vinyl cover and black vinyl back cover. Recent candidates have told me this all costs around $5-$7 per creative interview kit. Not much when it comes to what's at stake, right?

You'll never again wonder if you've impressed a hiring manager. You'll know for sure.

3rd Way to Answer the Fit Question ➡ Make it Personal

How many offices do you walk into that have pictures of kids, a spouse or a college degree? What about a recent golf tournament photo or an award?

People like people who are like them and that's who they hire. If you dress like them (attire), look like them (visual connection of the kit) and connect with them on a personal level, you're more likely to land the job. How do you make it personal? Read on.

As you follow the interviewer into his or her office, do a quick 5- to 10-second scan to find one or two personal items that you can connect with him or her on directly. Make sure it's something that you feel comfortable discussing and that doesn't give away too much information. For example, selecting a picture of a baby is a great way to make an immediate personal connection, yet you want to be careful that you avoid revealing your parental status.

You can make the personal connection by saying "That's a lovely baby photo. Is (s)he yours?" As the conversation unfolds, simply engage by saying that you love being an aunt/uncle rather than divulging your parental status. Why?

It may seem natural to connect with a fellow parent; however, it truly can and does affect many hiring decisions.

Better yet select a hobby-related photo such as golf, tennis, baseball or the like. Hobbies are a great way to get interviewers to let down their guard and make a personal connection with you, which keeps you top of mind after you leave and reminds them that they like you because you have something in common. Just ensure that you're being genuine.

Chapter 3.3 | Effective Preparation: Google, LinkedIn and the Like

Before you walk out the door or show up at the company's office, preparing for the interview will help you increase your chances of success—some people don't prepare enough. The days of the old job search game meant researching a company online was preparation enough for an interview. Spend 15 minutes fiddling around on their Website, read the "About Us" page, a bit about the services/products they offer and you'd be off and running.

In today's job search game, you need to prepare to give yourself an edge. I'm going to give you the tools and resources you need to walk in feeling ready to interview.

Researching the Company

According to <u>SCORE</u>, the resource partner for U.S. Small Business Association and Counselors to America's Small Business, you're likely interviewing with a company that your friends, family and former colleagues have never heard of before. Today, small businesses:

- Employ more than 50% of the U.S.'s private sector workforce (aka non-government employees)
- Represent 99.7% of all employer firms
- Hire 40% of all high-tech workers

And now it's time for really great news about working for a small business. Are you ready? Sixty-five percent of small businesses have a full-on casual workplace. Time to replace those trousers, with jeans, for good. Now that you know there's a very good likelihood you'll be interviewing with a small business rather than or in addition to one of the larger companies in the U.S., like Nestlé or Maytag, how do you prepare for and research them?

1. Google—**85% of hiring managers "Google" a candidate before or after an interview.**
   You want to Google the company too. You'll find their corporate Website as well as other press-related information and news articles on the company that are important to read prior to your interview.

2. Facebook—**45% of employers screen candidates using Facebook.**
   Does the company you're going to work for have a corporate Facebook page? If so, what do they use it for? Company promotions? Contests? Is it just informational? This tells you how socially networked the company is or isn't.

3. Twitter—**45% of employers screen candidates using Twitter.**
   This statistic tends to concern those candidates who have never used Twitter. No need to worry if you're new to Twitter. If a company is on Twitter, it'll likely show up in your Google search. It's a good idea, however, to double-check, which can be done by simply searching directly on Twitter's home page (see below, Figure 2.2).

Real-Life Testimonial

A candidate was extended an offer on a Friday to start the following Monday at a top competitor. After the offer was extended, the CEO of the company (who did said offer extending) Googled him and saw a picture of a newspaper article where the new hire had been arrested in a different state three years before. The offer was immediately recanted.

Figure 2.2

4. <u>Hoovers</u>—This is where you can find complete data on 65 million companies (and it's insanely easy to search). For free, you can get information such as:

   - Top three executives names, titles and ages, if available
   - Company's address, address and fax number
   - Competitive landscape
   - Other industry-related companies

- Description of company services and products

5. <u>Venture Beat Profiles</u>—If it's hard to find information about a company in question, this is a great place to grab details about small, new and emerging companies that have 5-50 employees and have accepted venture capital funds.

When you walk into an interview prepared with the profiles of senior management, competitors and the company's current social media engagement (or lack thereof), it makes a clear statement that you're confident, intelligent and put-together. You also show the employer that you know how to research his or her company and you're going to do what it takes to become part of not just any company but the right company.

Researching the Interviewers

Okay, you know what the company is all about. What do you know about the person you'll be talking with during the interview? When it comes to researching the interviewer, you can use some of the same aforementioned resources but in different ways.

1. <u>Google</u>—Remember those 85% of hiring managers who are Googling you? Go ahead and Google them. Find out what you can and beware: you can't forget what you see and read.

2. <u>Facebook</u>—If 45% of employers are screening you on Facebook, this means they have personal profiles and

you can find a potential personal connection point with an interviewer—an alma mater, a hobby in common or even a professional association to which you both belong. For some Facebook fans, the popular Farmville game may be a connection point. (I don't get it, but 77 million players a month can't be wrong.)

Just remember while you're job searching that if they're looking at you and you're looking at them, it's a good idea to lock down or even remove pictures and updates that are of a more personal nature. That trip to Vegas? Yes, those pictures.

3. Twitter—About 45% of employers screen candidates using Twitter. No need to worry if you're new to "Tweeting." If a company is on Twitter, simply search for it directly on Twitter's home page (see Figure 2.2).

Insider Tip: Without a person's Twitter "handle" (e.g., @adrianallames) it may take a few variations of their name to find them. Try multiple options (e.g., Adriana Llames, adrianallames, AdrianaLlames, adrianallames, Adriana Llames Chicago). The company's Website might also have a link to its Twitter page.

4. LinkedIn—This is where 65 million professionals across the world come together to network online, and that number is growing. If you're interviewing with someone, there's a good chance that one of your contacts knows that person or someone who knows

him or her. This applies to the six degrees of connection, which I delve into in chapter four.

LinkedIn is the only social network I strongly recommend to my career coaching clients. This is networking done well, and I love it. When I get a request to connect a colleague's friend or fellow colleague, I'm always happy to oblige. If the same request came via Facebook, there's only a 10% chance I'd respond the same way. Why? Because I use LinkedIn for business purposes, and I use Facebook for personal reasons. LinkedIn is known as a business and professional networking resource, whereas Facebook is known for fun and games, plain and simple.

You've done your research, prepared yourself and you're ready to head out the door and show hiring managers you belong.

Chapter 3.4 | Top 10 Toughest Interview Questions and Answering Them Confidently

"Tell me a little about yourself." This is the #1 toughest interview question as ranked by CNN.com, CareerBuilder.com and job seekers alike.

What's the winning job search interview answer? You already have it: your knock-out, powerful 30-second pitch, which is *the* best answer to give when asked this question. It gives the ideal combination of skills, experience, and accomplishments combined into a short, concise and clear, 30-second answer.

Insider Tip: The "Tell me a little about yourself" question is often asked by an interviewer who has done little to no preparation before your interview and is using the time to review your résumé. He or she is probably new to interviewing. Using your powerful 30-second pitch will capture his or her attention and show your confidence.

When it comes to job search success and interview techniques, knowing what questions you will face in the interview is only half the battle. I'm going to give you the advice and expert insight to help you answer these tough interview questions with coolness and ease.

Tough Question #2: Why did you leave your last job?

This is a great time to talk about your experience and skills. It's a bad time to give a laundry list of reasons you left. *Never, ever badmouth a former employer.*

Confidently Answering Question 2:

"My role at Company X was a great way to use my graphic design skills yet wasn't a good fit for my overall creativity. I realized that different companies have diverse roles just like people do, and I'm looking forward to bringing the full suite of my skills to fruition in a new role."

Tough Question #3: What are your weaknesses?

Today's job search candidates think this is a question of the past. I'm here to tell you it's alive and well! *Always give a weakness and wrap it with a strength.* Expose a vulnerability and be honest (organization, details, etc.?) and use an example to explain a way you have addressed *correcting the problem.*

Confidently Answering Question 3:

"I'm great at selling and cold-calling, but I'm not so strong when it comes to reporting. I know I have to do it, so I worked with our sales support person to help me build an automated report and put a reminder in my outlook to pull a report at 4 p.m. every day out of Salesforce. Sales is my thing; reporting is something I'm working on improving."

Tough Question #4: Where do you see yourself in five years?

It's hard for me to even imagine people asking this question in today's economic climate and yet it's still a top interview question and ranked as one of the top five toughest.

Avoid canned answers like, "I want to get in on the ground floor and work for your company so I can build my family at the same time as we build the company." If you said this to me while I was a recruiter, I would have had to fake my way through the rest of the interview—boring.

Confidently Answering Question 4:

Throw in a bit of light humor about the U.S. economic situation and then play up the company and your skill set at the same time.

"Given the economic climate as of late, I'm not sure anyone knows where they'll be in five years. Nonetheless, I want to secure a position with an industry-leading media agency like yours that can capitalize on my creativity and challenge me to continue growing professionally."

Tough Question #5: Why should we hire you?

Personally, I love this question. If you're confident—and by the time you're done reading *Career Sudoku: 9 Ways to Win the Job Search Game* you'll be one confident candidate—you will also love this question.

Actor Alec Baldwin gives the best advice as Blake in *Glengarry Glen Ross* when he says, "A-B-C. A-Always. B-Be. C-Closing. Always be closing." Always be selling YOU. This is your chance to sell yourself, so do it confidently. Let the interviewer know what sets you apart from other candidates.

Below, the answer demonstrates a problem-solving scenario. Employers don't like problems (poor efficiency that results in high costs). They like solutions (reduction of high costs via improved efficiency).

Confidently Answering Question 5:

"Why should you hire me? Because I'm a great manager and a savvy motivator. As a senior manager for the past three years at Apple Industries, I managed a team of seven and a budget of $450K. I'm proud to say that I was able to reduce our team's operating expenses by 22% through printing efficiencies, cross-training and scheduling changes. I engaged my team to help with the cost-reduction ideas, so in addition to reducing costs, it increased team morale."

Tough Question #6: What are your salary requirements?

Ah, an oldie but goody. Tough, tough, tough. This question is awful, uncomfortable and known as "the deal-breaker." That's exactly why recruiters and hiring managers ask it! When I discuss negotiation later, you'll learn more about why they ask it too. The basic premise is that there's a perception that the first person to throw out a number loses.

Confidently Answering Question 6:

"I'm most interested in the position, and while salary is important to me like it is to most people, I'd rather focus on what the company can offer from an overall compensation perspective."

If the interviewer pushes for a number, focus on a salary range. Never give a number when responding to this question.

"Given my experience, education and salary history, I'd like to stay on the higher end of the $60-$70K range, and while we haven't had the chance to discuss the budget for this position, given my research of the current market trends,

the company size and my market value, it seems reasonable. I'm happy to negotiate, of course. How does that fit with your budget for this position?"

Insider Tip: Prior to an interview, you can use salary calculators on Websites such as salary.com and payscale.com to determine your market value and find out the average, high and low payscales for your desired position. Knowledge is power, indeed.

Tough Question #7: When were you most satisfied in your last job?

Yeah, story time. This is a behavior-based question and is often asked when the interviewer is trying to get to know you as a person and how you will fit in with the company or team. Answer with a story about what you liked about your last position and how what you liked will transfer well into the position you're interviewing for right then.

Confidently Answering Question 7:

"When I was at 24/6 Technology, I was most satisfied when I was working directly with the clients during the sales calls and in presentations. That's one of the reasons I'm excited about this position. It looks as though I'll be able to spend a portion of my day with direct customer-facing duties."

Tough Question #8: How would others describe you?

For some, this answer is on the tip of the tongue and for others, it's difficult. If you ask colleagues and your manager for feedback on your performance then you know what to say. If you have recommendations from your contacts on LinkedIn or recommendation letters from former or current colleagues—which you should ascertain—review them for tidbits to use in this answer.

Confidently Answering Question 8:

"One of my colleagues at Jones Technology described me recently as someone who tackles projects head on and is as sweet as a cupcake. I'm not sure I'm that sweet, but it's nice to be known as effective and easy to work with at the same time. I'd be happy to provide you with additional comments, references or letters of recommendation so you can get firsthand feedback."

<u>Tough Question #9</u>: Chose three adjectives to describe you and tell me why you chose those three?

You won't see this on a top 10 list anywhere; however, you'll run into it more and more in different varieties. It's often worded as "describe your strengths." I've asked this question to candidates for more than nine years now, and every time I ask it, the candidate stops cold.

Prepare with a strong, confident and authoritative answer. Remember, this is all about YOU.

Confidently Answering Question 9:

"I would describe myself as smart, assertive and energetic. I selected smart because I pursued my Bachelor's degree and 30+ additional educational courses, including four from Harvard Business School's Management program, on my own, and I'm a quick learner. I chose assertive because when I decide I want something, whether it's a new deal to add to our client roster or a new car, I go after it and I do what it takes to get it. And last, I chose energetic because I get up with the sun and have an abundance of energy that seems to go and go—kind of like the Energizer bunny. And I'm often told I get a week's worth of work done in a day."

<u>Tough Question #10</u>: Do you have any questions for me?

Blank stare. That's what employers get most often when they ask this question. Hint: Blank stares are not good in an interview and they give away the fact that you're unprepared. Saying "no" implies a lack of interest, motivation and research for the position and company. Asking questions about salary, benefits or work schedule are basic and what any job candidate would ask.

This is about you winning the job search game—not just playing, so ask questions that get you real answers.

Confidently Answering Question 10:

Read on for a list of the top 25 questions to ask in an interview. They are grouped by topic to make it easy for you to select which ones you'd like to ask: culture, job specific, hiring manager, company related, interview timeline and next steps.

Chapter 3.5 | Top 25 Most Impressive Interview Questions (to Ask)

Imagine asking an interview question and having the hiring manager give you a look of surprise and say, "Great question." Hiring managers expect candidates to ask basic, bland or thoughtless questions (if they ask them at all).

When you prepare for your interview and ask questions that are thought-provoking, interesting and show you've done your research, you earn big points and impress the interviewer. Following are the top 25 most impressive interview questions.

Culture/Environment Questions

1. How would you describe the culture and work environment at the company?
2. How are decisions made within your organization?
3. What is the company's strategy for rewarding employees for performance excellence?
4. How do you inspire pride in your organization?
5. What three words would you use to describe the culture here at Company X?

Job-Specific Questions

6. What do you think the top three challenges will be in this position?

7. Do you expect travel to be a part of this position? If so, how often?

8. What are the main responsibilities of this position?

9. What is the extent of my authority to carry out these responsibilities?

10. Who will be my key associates and colleagues in this position?

11. Six months from now, how will you know you hired the right person in this position?

12. What objectives or standards will I be expected to meet or exceed?

13. If you had one piece of advice to give the person coming into this position, what would it be?

14. What three skills do you feel are the most important in this position?

15. How will my performance be measured in this position?

Hiring Manager-Specific Questions

16. What is your management style?

17. What are you personally looking for in a successful candidate?

18. What do you do to lead by example?

Company-Related Questions

19. Is the company open to trying innovative strategies or is it more about playing it safe?
20. What are some ways that you generate useful approaches to improve the way you do things?
21. When did you join Company X and what made you decide to join?
22. What do you like best about being part of Company X?

Interview Timeline/Next Steps

23. What is your timeline for interviewing and making a hiring decision?
24. When can I expect to hear from you or would you prefer that I call you?
25. Can you describe the hiring/interviewing process for this position? (This one may be used in conjunction with or instead of question #23.)

Insider Tip: "If you had one piece of advice to give the person coming into this position, what would it be?"—ask each person you interview with this question. The answers can provide great insight into the company culture, environment and the position as well.

Avoid surprises by asking at least five thoughtfully selected questions in every interview. You can ask each interviewer different questions or toss in a few of the same.

Mix it up to build a clear picture of this job.

Insider Tip: Use an 8 ½ x 11 pad folio that has a slot for your résumé on the left side and a legal pad on the right side. Write your questions for each interviewer on the legal pad.

What do you do if you're being interviewed on the phone? You can definitely ask these questions over the phone as well. And there are ways to master the phone interview....read on.

Chapter 3.6 | 10 Ways to Master the Phone Interview

The dreaded phone interview has become a regular part of today's hiring process. Why?

- Efficient use of time: 15-30 minutes per candidate vs. 60 minutes face-to-face
- Fiscally responsibly: interview out-of-town candidates without travel costs
- Highly effective: screen candidates that are "maybes" and move them to "yes" or "no" status quickly

While these benefits are nice for prospective employers, the phone interview can cause anxiety for many candidates. If you have a phone interview coming up, use these 10 tips to ace it:

1. Prepare.

Research the company just as you would if it were a normal, face-to-face interview at the company. Refer to the tips discussed earlier in this chapter.

2. Avoid distraction.

Keep yourself free of any distractions during the entire interview. Turn off e-mail, close your laptop; get a sitter for the kids, etc. Focus entirely on the interview and the interview alone.

3. Quiet is key.

There's nothing more distracting than being in an interview and having background noise—for either party. Take the phone call in a quiet location. If you're at your current job, use a private office or conference room and use common sense regarding who might be listening to you. Using your cellular phone—and your personal e-mail address when otherwise corresponding with the hiring manager, not your company e-mail address—is best.

4. Take notes.

Keep a notepad and pen with you during the interview and take notes on questions, answers, job description, follow-up interview dates/times, etc.

5. Have your calendar handy.

Imagine the best-case scenario: you're asked to come for an in-person interview next week. With your calendar in hand, you're ready to schedule it right away. Tuesday at 3 p.m. is great.

6. Ask questions.

This is a great reason to prompt them to bring you in for further interviews: *to answer your questions.* Prepare a list of three to five relevant, company-specific, position-specific questions to ask the interviewer.

7. Respect the time.

Your interviewer likely has quite a few phone interviews scheduled. If your time is nearing an end and you have questions left to ask, simply mention that you'd like to ask a few questions and you want to respect his or her time; allow them to take the lead.

8. Dress nicely.

Studies prove that if you dress nicely, you feel better. Dress as if you were interviewing in person. If you're afraid this will call attention at your casual office, wear a blazer and dress shirt with your jeans. There's always a way to kick it up a notch so you feel more professional. It will *show* in your voice.

9. Smile, smile, smile.

One of the oldest tricks in the book is to smile. Simple, right? Any good salesperson will tell you that you can *hear* a smile on the other side of the phone. Think of the last conversation you had with your best friend. Can you tell if he or she is smiling? Sure you can. My best friend can call me and when she asks how I'm doing, if I say, "I'm good" when I'm stressed, she'll say, "Then why aren't you smiling like you normally do?" She lives 1,500 miles away.

Remember to smile; people like to hire happy, positive, smiling employees.

10. Send a thank-you note.

This is the #1 thing candidates forget to do when it comes to phone and in-person interviews. *It's a simple touch that goes a long way.* How far will it take you? **Only 5% of candidates send thank-you notes, which means you stand out from 95% of the market.**

When it comes to sending thank-you notes, I get all kinds of questions about when to send them, what to say, if you can use e-mail, etc. The list of questions about thank-you notes and their importance goes on and on. Because the thank-you note will increase your job search success and have you stand out, I'm going to dedicate an entire sub-chapter to it.

Here you go: answers to all the questions you have about interview thank-you notes.

Chapter 3.7 | Follow-Up, Follow-Up, Follow-Up

Location, location, location is what real estate is all about, right? That's what they say. Buy the least expensive house in the most expensive neighborhood. By the way, I did this when I bought my first home and made a great profit with barely any upgrades. (Looking back, I think the one wall we painted might have actually been a downgrade…)

When it comes to interviewing, it's all about follow-up, follow-up, follow-up. I'm going to do this in a short question-and-answer format because it's that simple.

Q: Do you have to send a thank-you note?
A: No.

Q: Will sending a thank-you note increase my chances of landing the job?
A: Yes.

Q: **Why** is sending a thank-you note important?
A: Because 95% of people who interview do not send one, and when you do, you stand out in that little 5%.

Q: **When** do you send a thank-you note?
A: The same day you interview.

Q: **Who** do you send thank-you note(s) to?
A: Each person you interview with, including executive assistants who schedule interviews with C-level or senior

level executives. **Make sure to get a business card for every person you interview with.**

Q: **How** do you send a thank-you note?

A: I strongly recommend sending both a handwritten thank-you note and an e-mail.

- Postal mail doesn't get caught by spam filters.
- When was the last time you got a small, handwritten note? It catches your attention these days because it's infrequent.

Q: **What** do you write in a thank-you note?

A: A short, simple, personalized note should thank the person for spending time with you and for sharing his or her insights on the company and the position. Make each note personal and different.

Chapter Three | Impressive Interviews | Review

Chapter 3.1 | The First 8 Seconds
- Arrive promptly: 10 minutes before your interview.
- Wear appropriate attire.
- Give a medium-firm handshake.
- Use proper body language: 55% of communication is received from body language.

Chapter 3.2 | 3 Answers to the "Fit" Question
- Look the part: incorporate corporate colors into your wardrobe.
- Show them you belong using your creative interview kit.
- Make it personal: connect with the interviewer.

Chapter 3.3 | Effective Preparation
- Research the company via SCORE, Google, Twitter, Facebook, Hoovers, VentureBeatProfiles.
- Research the interviewer via Google, Facebook, Twitter, LinkedIn.

Chapter 3.4 | Top 10 Toughest Interview Questions and Answering Them Confidently
- Understand the #1 toughest question: "Tell me a little about yourself."
- Prepare and practice your answers.
- Give all answers with confidence and authority.

Chapter 3.5 | Top 25 Impressive Interview Questions (to ask)

- Prepare to ask at least five thoughtfully selected questions.
- Ask the #1 question: "If you had one piece of advice to give the person coming into this position, what would it be?"
- Use an 8 ½ x 11 pad folio to show you're prepared and ready to ask questions.

Chapter 3.6 | 10 Ways to Master The Phone Interview

- Prepare, avoid distraction, quiet is key.
- Take notes, have your calendar handy, ask questions.
- Respect time, dress nicely, smile.
- Send thank-you note(s).

Chapter 3.7 | Follow-Up, Follow-Up, Follow-Up

- Only 5% of candidates send a thank-you note—stand out.
- Send both a handwritten thank-you note and an e-mail *the same day*.
- Personalize your thank-you notes to each interviewer.

Ready to put your new interview skills to work? Great. Let's give you the tools to network—naturally and confidently—so you have the chance to impress hiring managers and land your new job.

CHAPTER FOUR

NETWORKING NATURALLY

	9		6			3		
				8	3			5
2					7			
	8					5		
3							4	
	1							2
		7						
1			5		9		6	
		4		3		7		

"80% of jobs are found through networking"
-ABC News

Networking is one of the most important—if not *the* most important—activity you need to master in order to be a truly successful job seeker and to land a job in any economy.

By the time you finish reading this chapter, you'll have the tools and resources to network naturally and know how to find networking events and what to say when you arrive.

Chapter 4.1 | What is Job Search Networking?

Networking is the art of building alliances and relationships. It starts long before a job search. If you have relationships and friendships you've built in recent years, alliances with colleagues at work—that's networking. You already know how to network, *naturally*, and I bet you didn't even realize it.

If you've been thinking that job search networking is about contacting everyone you know and asking if they know of any job openings, you're not alone. This is a common misperception and it's the #1 *myth* about networking for a new job.

Chapter 4.2 | Finding the "Hidden" Job Market

Kelly Pate of the *Denver Post* wrote in her article, "Everyday People Key in Job Networking" (March 30, 2003), that "Friends, friends of friends, a barber, a neighbor and former co-workers are often the best resources for job seekers, especially in a market with far more people out of work than job openings, job placement experts say."

You're networking when you:

- Attend professional or trade association meetings
- Talk to fellow parents at your children's sporting or music events
- Volunteer for a local 5K charity run
- Visit with other members of your social clubs
- Talk to your neighbors
- Chat up the neighbor standing in line at the coffee shop
- Strike up a conversation with the person sitting next to you in the dentist office
- Catch up with your stylist while getting your hair cut
- Mingle over a glass of wine before your book club starts

While 80% of jobs are found through networking, 27.3% of all new hires are referrals (i.e., employee referrals). Imagine yourself in the hiring manager's shoes and receiving three names of potential candidates. Each candidate has similar qualifications, education and expertise. One of the candidates, Robert, was referred to you by your good friend, Kate, who you have dinner with every Wednesday. Kate's talked about Robert quite a bit, and you're looking forward to meeting him. When you do, you spend 15 minutes of the one-hour interview talking "shop" and the rest talking about Kate, other mutual interests and favorite dinner places around town. The other two candidates now seem a bit boring. You decide to hire Robert, of course.

Can you see how this scenario works in real life? The referred candidate always has the upper hand in the job search game and, most likely, finds a job through a friend rather via a job board.

According to Paula Ledbetter Sellergren of LedbetterPR.com, public relations today is not just about working with media to feature a product or service. It's about *creating a conversation*—beyond hype or a trend. Think of networking as a public relations initiative about you. Craft your YOU brand, supplement it with the right materials (résumé, business card) and communicate the proper messages to complete your image in the public realm (a.k.a the job search game).

Let others who know you — those who know your brand —spread the good word about what they've experienced. But in order for people to be talking about you, you need to be talking with them first. Get out there.

> ### Real-Life Scenario
>
> Anna hosted a spaghetti dinner at her home in Aurora, Colo., for 30+ friends. Since she's a less-than-stellar cook, she made the salad and left the sauce to the experts while she poured wine and mingled, getting to know her new guests. After five or so introductions, it suddenly felt as though she was hosting an open house for the company Level 3 Communications.
>
> Level 3 executives met who they wanted over wine, chatted them up over salad, had informal interviews over spaghetti, and by dessert they had exchanged business cards with three other guests. Within a month, Level 3 had stolen two of US West's top performers in sales and HR, one of whom was Anna.

Would you expect to meet a job lead, or future boss, at your neighbor's spaghetti dinner? Probably not. Yet that's exactly what happened to Anna and another colleague, and it's what's happening every night in homes and dining rooms across the country.

From spaghetti dinners to book clubs and social gatherings of the like, people meeting people is the definition of a networking event. What I want to encourage you to do is get out there. Log off your computer, lace up your shoes and get out and meet people.

I live in a neighborhood where it's hard to walk down the street without five or ten people saying hello and knowing who you are; it's one of the things I love about my neighborhood. The other night, my better half, Jim, and I went for a walk with the intention of ending at a favorite local dinner spot, Le Colonial. As we approached the restaurant, there was a line that started 25 feet before Le Colonial, covered the lovely patio area and wrapped down the block and around the corner. Jim looked at me and said, "What is this?" I knew immediately what it was. Everyone dressed in black with one bit of color and standing in line not talking to one another. It's a networking event.

We decided to walk another four blocks down the street to check out another local restaurant, and when we came back 15 minutes later, those people in line were all still waiting there—not talking to each other—hoping the doors would open soon so they could "network." At this point, I starting laughing and had to cross the street so I didn't hurt anyone's feelings. Were they serious? Who stands in line for 20+ minutes saying nothing so you can get inside and then say something to the people you've been standing in line with?

Here's what I recommend you do if you ever find yourself in a similar situation. Start chatting up a storm in that line, get as many cards as you can by asking, "What do you do and how can I help you?" Your networking will get started and will probably finish before those doors ever open. Who knows? You might be off to dinner with five to seven new friends rather than in a room of 100 strangers.

Consider the odds of who you would want to talk to if you're in that situation: a person standing silent or a person who's chatting with two other people? A smiling, friendly person is far more approachable, creating an effect of more people approaching them.

Every one of those people came there for one reason: to meet other people. But not one person in that line was speaking to anyone else. No one. Insane? Yes. Normal? Yes. I've been to hundreds of networking events, and I see this nearly every time.

No one likes to network if it's forced.

Networking Events: The Ugly Truth

Show me someone who says they like networking events and I'll show you a liar or jokester. No one likes networking events; they're unnatural, borrrrrrring and completely uncomfortable. There's a reason why the majority of networking events are after hours…and include alcohol. It's not because you work during the day; these events are to create business-related leads, after all. The alcohol helps people relax enough to digest the anxiety of it all.

The ugly truth about networking events is that they work. If they didn't, no one would attend them and they wouldn't be happening nearly every Tuesday and Thursday night in every major city around the U.S. With that said, in the aforementioned list of where you network the most, I intentionally excluded "networking events" from the list.

There are focused job-seeker networking events; however, I've found them to be less productive than other forms of networking and less fruitful in terms of gaining actual job leads.

Great networking events for job seekers are:

- **Industry-related events**

  - Hiring managers attend these to keep up to date on industry topics
  - You look like you're staying current on industry news and events
  - Great way to connect with recruiters in your desired industry
  - Employees from the company you want to work at will attend and have inside info on hiring managers

- **Professional organizations**

  - Associations on the Net: The Internet Public Library site lists organizations that have an online presence so you can explore groups you might want to join.
  - Gateway to Associations Online: The American Society of Association Executives (ASAE) provides a comprehensive directory to Websites of business and professional associations.
    - If you're in the non-profit industry, ASAE is a wonderful resource with the top executives of nearly every association in the country. Find the association you want to work for and network your way

directly into it by sending a letter, e-mail, or better yet, call the CEO directly.

- o <u>WEDDLE's Association Directory</u>: This site lists thousands of associations by their primary professional/occupational focus and/or industry of interest.

- **Social Organizations and Clubs**

  - o See the Networking Resources Appendix for a list of organizations.
  - o Religious organizations and communities such as churches, temples, etc., are great places to network.
  - o Book clubs are popular these days—arrive early and network before it begins.
  - o Are you a member of a rock-climbing club? Network before the climb. (Focus on the rocks during the climb; I don't want you to get hurt!)
  - o Need to find a social club or organization to join? Log on to <u>MeetUp</u>.com and search for groups in your area that interest you.

- **Coffee Shops**

  - o Starbucks has become my new c'office* simply because the networking, and let's face it, the coffee is better than in my office
  - o Caribou
  - o Seattle's Best Coffee
  - o Intelligentsia

○ Log off, lace up and hit your local coffee shop. These are the new social networks folks. Face time is seven to times more effective than phone time according to author and CEO of Networlding Melissa Giovagnoli.

c'office is a term I developed that means coffee office.

Chapter 4.3 | How to Network Naturally for a New Job

People hire people, so you have to get out there and meet people. How do you do that?

There are five basics you need covered to make networking effective. Most job seekers overlook at least one, if not more, of these five basic needs, creating ineffective networking experiences.

1. **Business cards**

    Make it easy for people to reach you, give you job leads and call you for an interview. Your card should have:

    - Name
    - Title
      (e.g., marketing guru, operational black belt, award-winning graphic designer)
    - Phone number
    - E-mail address (keep it professional, avoid crazy or group e-mail addresses)
    - Include your UVP as a tagline (optional)
    - Keep your card design professional, clean, fresh and organized

    To get business cards for free (you pay shipping and handling) and use a professional template design, try sites such as VistaPrint.com.

2. Powerful 30-second pitch (aka selling YOU)

"What do you do?," "What are you looking for?," "How can I help you?" questions—be prepared, confident and natural.

3. Résumé

Never bring a résumé to a networking meeting. Why? It seems too desperate and removes any reason to follow-up. You have a business card to provide your contact information and so do they. Ask for a card, give them yours and send thank-you notes after your meetings *with your résumé included.*

4. Pad folio

When you walk into a networking meeting (one-on-one) with an 8 ½ x 11 black pad folio, it creates a professional, organized and prepared appearance. Your pen, paper and cards are at your fingertips, and you can prepare a list of questions in advance on the paper inside.

5. Thank-You notes

As with interviewing, sending thank-you notes is an important part of networking. When someone takes time out of his or her busy day to meet with you and provide advice, job leads or feedback, send a personal, handwritten thank-you note. Five percent of people send interview thank-you notes, and even less send networking thank-you notes. If you can afford it, include a small gift card (e.g., $5 Starbucks).

With these five items in your back pocket, you're ready to hit the networking pavement. What's up next?

The Fabulous List of 50

I created this exercise more than 10 years ago, and it's still one of the most effective, popular (and complained-about) exercises with my career coaching clients today. The template below was designed in Word, but you can use any program you'd like, including my favorite: pen and paper. Remember that you'll want to be able to update the list on a regular basis and refer back to it often.

adrianallames®

Fabulous list of 50 Networking Exercise

This exercise is designed launch your job search networking. When job searching, networking is the most critical key to success. Start by listing 50 people you know and have contact information for (phone number, email address). Rank each one with the following number system:

1 = Very comfortable with this person, Easy to call them

2 = Comfortable enough with this person, prefer to e/mail them

3 = Hardly know this person, uncomfortable with contacting them directly

Name	Ranking (1, 2 or 3)
1.	
2.	
3.	
4.	
5.	
6.	
7.	
8.	
9.	
10.	
11.	
12.	
13.	
14.	
15.	
16.	

17.	
18.	
19.	
20.	
21.	
22.	
23.	
24.	
25.	
26.	
27.	
28.	
29.	
30.	
31.	
32.	
33.	
34.	
35.	
36.	
37.	
38.	
39.	
40.	
41.	
42.	
43.	
44.	
45.	
46.	
47.	
48.	
49.	
50.	

This list is the beginning of a new process in your career transition — networking naturally.

Continue the exercise until you reach 50 names and rank each name 1, 2 or 3. Now it's time to gather the contact information for each of the 50 people on your list.

Once you have the contact information for at least 10 people, **begin networking**. Call a "1" on your list and explain what you're doing. Remember, 1s are people you're very comfortable talking to and they'll be the easiest to begin this process with.

Goal: Ask each person on your list of 50 to provide you with the names and contact information of a few other people that you should reach (two names minimum). These names then get added to your list, and it should grow to 75 and then 100 quickly. All the names you add will be ranked as 3s. Once you get to your second week of networking through this list, you'll find that you have a lot of 3s. At this point, make sure that at least half of your networking appointments/calls/meetings are with 3s.

Note that this can be a bit uncomfortable in the beginning. As Maria Shriver once said, *"Do one thing every day that scares you."* This is worth it and if you keep at it, it'll be what makes the job search game a winning one. This will work if you do it. It *will*. It has for 12 years for my career coaching clients, from a former Fortune 50 CTO to a client relations rep in Madison, Wisconsin.

What do you say? Following are guidelines and suggestions to get you started comfortably with your networking. Be confident that once you make the first few calls you'll be off and running. You'll have your own script that will feel normal and ooze authority.

Use your smile to your advantage. Sometimes it helps to put a mirror next to the phone to remind you to smile (I still use this trick when I'm coaching clients). Just remember to be friendly, specific and make it easy to say yes. You'll have the best chance at success if you choose a location that's convenient for the person you want to network with and a time you know will be relatively easy for him or her.

Sample phone call:

"Hi, this is Adriana. I'd like to grab a cup of coffee with you and reconnect. How does your calendar look on Tuesday at 9 a.m. for us to meet at the Starbucks on Division and Dearborn?"

Sample voice mail:

"Hey, Sharon, it's Andy. I know it's been a bit since we chatted last. I'd love to grab a cup of coffee and reconnect. Let me know how your schedule looks next Tuesday, the 25th, at 9 a.m. It's been forever since I stopped in at Buttery Café for a latte, and I'll be in the neighborhood. My treat. I'm at 312.555.1951." (Be sure to state your phone number clearly and slowly.)

<u>Sample e-mail message #1</u>:
(Double-check spelling and grammar.)

Subject line: Coffee & Conversation

Hi Robert,

I hope you're doing well and enjoying the warm weather that's finally arrived; I thought winter was never going to end this year. It's been a while since we last connected, and I'd love to get together this week to talk shop. How's your schedule look this Wednesday morning to grab coffee at Stella's on Pearl Street?

Looking forward to catching up and hearing how the new house has been coming along.

Talk soon,
Bree

———

Sample e-mail message #2:
(Double-check spelling and grammar.)

Subject: Referral from Paula Lestrean

Good morning, Felice,

    I was given your name and contact information by Paula Lestrean, who's a good friend of mine and former colleague at Lenovo. Paula told me that you're a marketing genius there at Dell and know anyone and everyone when it comes to who's who in marketing and PR. I would love to buy you a cup of coffee, glass of wine—pick your poison—if you'd give me 20 minutes of your expert, savvy knowledge. How does Thursday at 4 p.m. work for your calendar?

    Thank you for considering my request, and I look forward to meeting you in person. Paula just raved about you and the amazing impact you've had on the Dell brand.

Take care,
Candace

————

    You will notice that both e-mails have a more informal tone. When you approach someone in a friendly (but not *too* friendly and casual) manner the message is received that way. If you write or call from a desperate or nervous state, then it'll be received as such and you're less likely to get a positive response. Be confident in your networking. People do want to help you.

Six Degrees of Connection: The Best Networking

The best job search networking is directly via people you know and the people they know; we are all connected. After I opened my first company, 6 Degrees, people would ask me what I did for a living. I would say, "I'm the CEO of 6 Degrees" and get one of two responses.

1. "I've heard of your company. You guys do…"

This response always got me to smile since I knew they didn't know who the heck we were and yet I loved that our brand had that kind of name recognition.

2. "Great name; it's like the 'six degrees of separation,' right?"

This would prompt me to say, "I prefer to think of it as the 'six degrees of connection.' I see us as all interconnected to one another."

Either response was a gateway to discuss why the concept was important for them, and it's just as important for you in your job search.

> **Real-Life Scenario**
>
> Your ideal job is being the executive producer of "The Suze Orman Show" on CNN. You know after reading *Career Sudoku: 9 Ways to Win the Job Search Game* that 80% of jobs are landed through networking and 27% of new hires are from employee referrals.
>
> Your goal is to meet face-to-face with one of the current executive producers of the show and to meet Suze Orman personally. You've given yourself 30 days to accomplish this goal.
>
> As a visual learner, I like to use charts and pictures to illustrate a point. Read on for a graphical representation of how six degrees of connection can make your goal a reality.

The premise of six degrees of connection is that anyone else in the world is within six people of you (aka you can reach them by connecting to five other people).

You can reach the people you want to network with or meet directly—that means an e-mail to their personal inbox, a phone call to them live, mail on their desk or better yet, a face-to-face meeting—simply by finding the one person in your network who knows one person who knows one other person who knows another person who knows the very good friend, neighbor or colleague of the person you're interviewing with or hoping to interview with eventually.

YOU

1st Degree: Josh
(Friend and former colleague who you remember has a friend in TV)

2nd Degree: Kevin (Josh's friend)
(Kevin works at CNBC in the PR department)

3rd Degree: Carol (Kevin's girlfriend)
(Carol also works in the PR dept. at CNBC and knows Kristin, Suze Orman's head of PR)

4th Degree: Kristin (Carol's colleague)
(Kristin knows Suze very well and one of the show's creative directors, Annie. She'll be happy to talk with you personally about the show and make the introduction to Annie.)

5th Degree: Annie (Kristin's friend and colleague)
Annie works closely with Ken, your interviewer, and is happy to give you the inside scoop. She also thinks it's a great idea to meet with Suze personally and will help you set it up.

Chapter Four | Networking Naturally | Review

Chapter 4.1 | What is Job Search Networking?

- Networking is the art of building alliances and relationships.
- Networking is not contacting everyone you know and asking for a job.

Chapter 4.2 | Finding the "Hidden" Job Market

- Talk with friends, neighbors and fellow parents.
- Attend spaghetti dinners, frequent social clubs and professional organizations' events.
- Networking events have their place; they do work.
  - o Yes—27.3% of new hires are from employee referrals.

Chapter 4.3 | How to Network Naturally for a New Job

- Bring your five basic needs:
  - o business cards, résumés, powerful 30-second pitch, pad folio, thank-you notes
- Roll out the Fabulous List of 50
- Understand the six degrees of connection concept
  - o You are six people away from the person you want to reach.

Networking in person is great to connect with people face-to-face, but what about the world of social networking that has exploded globally? How do you network successfully on Twitter or Facebook or LinkedIn? Do you really even need to use social networks? What's the real growth and reach of these social media networks anyway?

Social networking platforms have tools, resources and even advice for you, as a job seeker, that make them an effective resource and necessary platform for you to network. **To win the job search game, you need to learn how to harness the power of social media.** Using the networking naturally tools you learned, I'm going to break down the social media sphere for you and show you how to take advantage of the top networks. Let's go.

CHAPTER FIVE

SOCIAL NETWORKING STRATEGIES

	9		6			3		
				8	3			5
2					7			
	8					5		
3				5			4	
	1							2
		7						
1			5		9		6	
	4		3			7		

"85% of hiring managers Google a candidate before or after an interview."

— Wall Street Journal (*wsj.com*)

"45% of employers use Twitter and Facebook to screen job candidates."

— CareerBuilder.com *(by Harris Interactive)*

Social networking will grow from $965M in 2007 to a projected $2.4B by the end of 2012, according to Marketing Charts. According to Forrester, U.S. interactive marketing will hit nearly $55B by 2014 and will grow at a compound annual growth rate of 17%, from 12% overall ad spending in 2009 to 21% over the next five years.

If companies are spending advertising and marketing dollars on social media—and they clearly are—they want employees who understand the importance and value of social media in today's competitive market. Recruiters must be able to use Twitter, LinkedIn, Google, Facebook and a suite of other online resources to attract the best talent available in today's market.

You may not even know if you're being scoped out by a company, competitor, hiring manager or recruiter. Your Facebook page is being viewed, your LinkedIn profile is being peeked at and your name is being searched on Google. Absolutely.

When you're done reading this chapter, you'll be Internetworking—you'll know how to keep up with and take advantage of the social media sphere for your job search, including how to use Twitter, LinkedIn, Google and Facebook.

Chapter 5.1 | Twitter for Job Seekers

When someone said anything about a "Tweet," it used to refer to a living, breathing bird; that was until a noisy social networking-engine-that-could named Twitter came along. Twitter began as a sketch on a legal pad by Jack Dorsey in 2006 during a creative slump-busting, daylong brainstorming session held by board members of the podcasting company Odeo.

Twitter is what is called a micro blogging site. Micro blogging is a form of blogging; a micro blog differs from a traditional blog in that its content is typically much smaller in both actual size and aggregate file [character] size (Wikipedia.org).

These images may be subject to copyright and trademark and are only used for educational purposes in this book.

How Twitter Works

To post a Tweet, you need an account, which is free and easy to get. You log on to Twitter.com, register and start Tweeting. Tweets are text-based posts of up to 140 characters. They're displayed on your profile page and seen by your "followers" (aka fellow Twitter subscribers who are friends, colleagues and even strangers). There are many view-related restrictions for privacy, and they're all explained at Twitter.com.

You can search Twitter for free without an account (see Figure 2.2, Chapter 3). Both companies and individuals can register for accounts, which is why it has become a virtual online recruiting haven and reference-checking playground for companies in today's job market. A free tool to find candidates who are social media savvy? Employers have been all over it since 2009, and candidates who are registered and using it wisely are benefiting.

Twitter's Reach and Growth

Twitter has grown exponentially since 2007 when, at the popular Austin, TX-based music festival South by Southwest (SXSW), Tweets tripled from 20,000 to 60,000. By the end of 2007, about 500,000 Tweets per quarter were posted, and in the first quarter of 2010, *four billion* Tweets were posted! In March 2010, Twitter reported 1,500% growth in the number of registered users, 500% growth in the number of employees (sounds like a good place to be networking for a job if you're in San Francisco near Folsom St.), and more than 70,000 registered apps had been developed for the site.

Relevance to You as a Job Seeker

You want to be using Twitter four distinct ways to win the job search game:

1. Source new positions and opportunities—To get you going, here are some search terms to type in the Twitter search bar:

   i. #jobs or #jobsearch

   ii. #hiring listed 17 jobs in five states under these Twitter IDs:
       — jobschicago
       — ZuluJobsMN
       — michiganonline
       — JohnstonWake
       — Dandyprojectjob
       — alaskaonline
       — ZuluJobsMS

   iii. Use your city name followed by the word "jobs" (e.g., Madison jobs, Denver jobs). If you get zero results, put a space between the two words and try it again. Twitter can be particular.

2. Get free career advice—I post free interview, résumé and career tips exclusively via my Twitter account. Feel free to join the conversation with my other followers: @adrianallames. Search terms specific to your job search needs: "interview advice," "resume tips," "resume advice," "job interview," etc.

i. #resume #interview #unemployed—(these terms are called hashtags—Internet jargon you don't need to understand—because of the "#" in front of the search term. Hashtags will list any result in your desired category.)

I dropped the "e" accents in "résumé," by the way.

3. I consider online networking via Twitter to be third in terms of useful and relevant for you as a job seeker.

Since your ultimate goal is to land a job and Twitter can quickly overwhelm the even savviest of social networkers, I recommend focusing on networking specific to the jobs you find.

First, find who posted the job on Twitter. Contact him or her and ask who the hiring manager is. This works 25% of the time. For the other 75%, use other social networks that you'll understand by the end of this chapter (e.g., LinkedIn) and tools (Hoovers, VentureBeatProfiles.com) to find the hiring manager and get a personal introduction. Remember, 27.3% of new hires are from employee referrals according.

Your goal is to network yourself as far as you can so you never send a résumé to HR—except as a courtesy, of course. Land your résumé into *specific* human hands and use Twitter as a way to find the name.

4. Impress prospective employers—**Forty-five percent of employers screen candidates using Twitter**, and it's easy to do with the search feature. Here are guidelines to keep your Tweets job-search friendly:

    i. Never badmouth an interview or interviewer.

    ii. Post only positive comments about yourself. Remember, you're a brand.

    iii. Avoid Tweeting negative or too much information.
(e.g., "Oops, showed up 10 mins late for interview," "Did phone intv while blow-drying cat")

    iv. Tweet on a regular basis—three times/day is a good schedule

    v. Mix it up between professional, job-search friendly and personal
(e.g., reTweet job search advice to help other job seekers, Tweet an update about success with a recent position, finish the day with a Tweet about a great dinner you made or enjoyed)

Tweeting can be much easier than it seems if you remove the pressure and add fun to it. Most important, Twitter is a virtual world of information for you as a job seeker and *it's all free.*

Insider Tip: Use a free Twitter app like SocialOomph.com or Twuffer.com to pre-schedule your Tweets. They'll post to your Twitter account on the date/time you set, no matter where you are.

Chapter 5.2 | Facebook Job Search Strategies

"It's not personal. It's business"
— Don Lucchesi, *The Godfather*

According to a May 21, 2010, article about Facebook in *Time* magazine, Facebook will "log its 500 millionth active citizen" in the summer of 2010.

If you're over age 13, it's likely you've at least heard of Facebook. What's unlikely is that you thought it would become part of your job search. Although Facebook is beloved by youth, it reaches a very wide audience. Forty-eight percent of visitors have kids under 17 and 29% have kids 13-17; 62% earn an annual income of more than $60,000 and 55% of users are women (Quantcast.com).

The reason Facebook targets youth may be because of how it was developed. When he was a sophomore at Harvard University, founder Mark Zuckerberg originally invented "Facemash" and transformed it into what we know it as today (Wikipedia.org).

At this point, you know that 45% of employers use Facebook, along with Twitter, to screen job candidates. What does that mean to you? Let's dig into what Facebook is all about and then find out how to have fun on the site while winning the job search game.

These images may be subject to copyright and trademark and are only used for educational purposes in this book.

How Facebook Works

Facebook is a social networking Website where users, who register for free, join work- or college-related networks, add friends, colleagues and even strangers, send them messages, write on their "Walls" (pages where people post comments) and post videos as well as pictures.

Users update their personal profiles with fan pages, details about relationship status, etc. It can be a highly personal social networking site, and privacy on it is always changing, so it's important to get a handle on the privacy settings once you open your account.

In addition to individual users, Facebook has been extremely successful at developing company-specific pages. It's free for a company to have a page on Facebook; major brands like Coca-Cola have pages; e.g., Diet Coke, Coke Studio and Coke Zero. Hyatt uses its page entirely for Hyatt Hotels and Resorts Careers. Users have the option to "like" a company or service, thus becoming part of an online fan base.

Facebook's Reach and Growth

In the U.S., Facebook's user base grew from 42 million to 103 million in 2009, representing a 144.9% growth rate. The 35+ demographic is now the largest group on Facebook, comprising more than 30% of its entire base. The 55+ demographic grew by 922.7% in 2009. (Statistics are from Facebook.com and may differ from third-party reports such as Quantcast.)

As a company, Facebook has grown and transformed; its days of being run in a Harvard University dorm room are long over as Facebook now employs more than 1,200 people headquartered in Palo Alto, Calif.

Relevance to You as a Job Seeker

Despite companies that use Facebook for recruiting (e.g., Hyatt Hotels and Resorts), Facebook is still primarily a personal social utility for individuals and a marketing/promotional tool for companies.

1. Use Facebook for success as a job search utility—Focus your search terms, such as "Chicago jobs" "Los Angeles jobs" or "Atlanta jobs" when using the search bar (see Figure 2.4 above).

2. Use Facebook to network—You already know how to use Facebook when it comes to researching an interviewer; now you can use the power of the 'Net to network. Use Facebook's "Friend Finder" feature to reconnect with college friends, mates from elementary school, neighborhood friends you grew up with and even colleagues from former companies.

Real-Life Testimonial

Kim, who moved from Chicago to Malibu, Calif., reconnected with her childhood friend, Tricia, on Facebook. Kim was looking for a new job in the Los Angeles area and Tricia, who worked in online media, had quite a few clients in town. Tricia made e-mail introductions between Kim and three of her clients. Kim quickly followed up with phone calls and landed two interviews.

3. Use Facebook wisely—If 45% of employers are screening you on Facebook, it means they're on it regularly and looking at you. When job searching, apply the same professional filter you do to your résumé and interviews to Facebook Wall posts, photo albums and all other "unlocked" areas. If you don't want a prospective employer to see it, don't post it. Mind your privacy settings.

Real-Life Testimonial

In January 2008, Kate went on a two-week trek across Costa Rica with 10 friends and afterward they all posted their pictures on Facebook. The trip included an afternoon kayaking excursion to an island off the coast of Sumara, and given the hot, tropical day, the girls on the trip donned their bikinis to hit the kayaks for a sun-filled workout.

Fast forward two years and Kate's looking for a senior director of recruiting position. She got a call from the vice president at a worldwide staffing firm who interviews her over the phone. Near the end of the conversation, he begins to ask her about Costa Rica. She's happy to engage in personal conversation, knowing it'll help them connect. When she asks how he knows she went to Costa Rica, he replies that he saw her photos on Facebook and even comments that the kayaking trip "looked like a lot of fun." Thankfully, the conversation was via phone because Kate flushed red—fast.

Sometimes it may feel slightly creepy to know people are looking for and at you online—but it's a fact in today's job search game: Facebook is business, not personal.

Chapter 5.3 | Google and Your Job Search Strategy

Twelve years is how long Google has been in our lives and yet I don't know how I ever functioned without it, do you? The Google app is downloaded on my BlackBerry and I use it for every bit of knowledge I need, from a person's age to a restaurant address or the day's weather forecast. I even text Google (46645) to get phone and address information on the go. I am a self-proclaimed Google addict. So thank you, Larry Page and Sergey Brin, for developing this world-famous search engine that makes my life easier. Even seeing the image makes me happy. I feel as though the world is at my fingertips...and so do employers.

These images may be subject to copyright and trademark and are only used for educational purposes in this book.

How Google Works

Go to Google.com, enter any search term you want and voilà! Their little search engine "spiders" crawl the Web and find any and every Website related to your search term. It's fabulous—or is it?

Google's Reach and Growth

Google can translate into 41 languages, covering 98% of the languages read by Internet users, and handles nearly 250 million searches per day, which is approximately 70% of all search traffic. There isn't a way to get an exact number; however, it's safe to say that Google is still the largest search engine on the Web and will remain the biggest for years to come at the aggressive rate it's acquiring companies and growing. As of March 2008, Google has acquired a total of 51 companies; acquisitions include high-profile companies like AOL, YouTube and DoubleClick, which Google purchased for $3.1B.

Relevance to You as a Job Seeker

Eighty-five percent of hiring managers Google a candidate before or after an interview. As you read in the real-life testimonial in chapter three, even after an offer is extended, a hiring manager has the option to withdraw it if he or she finds something questionable about you online. Google is one of the places that a questionable item may be found. What can you do?

1. Know what Google's got on you—Set up a Google Alert on yourself at www.google.com/alerts. In the search term box, enter your name (e.g., Adriana Llames). Select comprehensive for the type of alert. Choose a frequency (e.g., daily). Enter your e-mail address. You're all set. You'll get the alert and know what Google's got on you.

2. Ensure accuracy—When your daily alert arrives in your e-mail, read it and ensure the information is accurate.

3. Correct inaccurate or damaging information— If you find it, so will a potential employer.

Contact the source and have it corrected or removed immediately. (Removal may take some time as Google's cache—more Internet jargon you don't need to understand—updates and clears.)

Chapter 5.4 | Linking In to a Powerful Job Search Network

More than 65 million professionals in 200 countries use LinkedIn.com to exchange information, ideas and opportunities. When it comes to the social media sphere and social networks, LinkedIn is *the* social network for professional use and the preferred network used by business executives around the world.

Formed in 2003, LinkedIn turned seven years old on May 3, 2010, shortly after it reported hosting 65 million professionals. As an avid (nearly daily) user, I'm thankful to Reid Hoffman and Allen Blue for co-founding this not-so-little social network. You'll be thankful, too, when you find out the abundance of free information, contacts, advice and jobs on it.

Linked in.

These images may be subject to copyright and trademark and are only used for educational purposes representing the author's personal profile on LinkedIn.

How LinkedIn Works

Go to LinkedIn.com and enter the first and last name of a professional you want to find. You'll get a brief overview profile page that shows the number of connections and recommendations the person has on the site. To view his or her entire LinkedIn profile, you need to join. It's easy and free. Simply complete your name, e-mail and select a password. You now have access to search all 65 million professionals—and you can connect to them.

LinkedIn's Reach and Growth

Now in 200 countries with more than 50% of its members outside the U.S., LinkedIn offers the site in English, French, German, Italian, Portuguese and Spanish. In just seven short years, the company has grown to more than 500 employees (you might want to apply here) and is located at 2029 Stierlin Ct. in Mountain View, Calif. It added advertising to its repertoire of products, staying on the leading edge of connecting people and businesses worldwide.

Relevance to You as a Job Seeker

Every time a client calls and tells me he or she has an interview, the first question I ask is, "Have you looked up their LinkedIn profile?" The uses for this powerful, information-filled tool are near limitless. Let's look at a few ways right now:

1. Your profile—Similar to your résumé yet only viewable to LinkedIn members, this highlights your professional accomplishments and allows you to write a summary (aka objective). I recommend including your education. Keep it streamlined, focused on facts, figures, and results, results, results.

2. Recommendations—The best LinkedIn profiles have recommendations. You can request a recommendation ("Endorse Me") from anyone in your network. I've endorsed former colleagues, vendors, clients and managers. Recruiters regularly search for profiles that meet their criteria and have three or more recommendations. Think of this as a virtual reference letter.

3. Job postings—Employers and recruiters know the caliber of candidates on LinkedIn.com is above the level of those on Monster.com or CareerBuilder.com; that's why they choose to post jobs here. LinkedIn Jobs also has postings exclusive to the site.

4. Groups—In addition to joining the site, you can join groups, which can be used for networking and asking expert advice. Many of them include group-specific job postings as well.

   - Join the group for your alma mater.
   - See if your former employer has a group and join.
   - Look for industry associations (e.g., Interactive Bureau of Advertising (IBA), SHRM, etc.).
   - **You can join my group: Job Search Success Boot Camp.** Just type it in the search bar.

5. Expert advice and answers—In the Questions and Answers area, many experts (including me) post advice and answers for free. Ask a question in any one of the many categories (job search, résumé writing, etc.) and you'll get responses almost instantly.

6. Events—Check the "Events Calendar" for local events related to networking, job search, career fairs or other group-related events in your area. You can even search what's going on in an area you want to relocate to or are interested in networking near.

Chapter Five | Social Networking Strategies | Review

Chapter 5.1 | Twitter for Job Seekers

- Yes—45% of employers use Twitter and Facebook to screen job candidates.
- Search for job postings, career experts and free advice with terms such as #jobs, #jobsearch, #resume, #interviewing, #hiring.
- Impress prospective employers with your Tweets.
  - o Mix it up by including professional and personal information.
  - o Avoid sharing negative or too personal information.
- Share when you're away with apps like socialoomph.com or twuffer.com.

Chapter 5.2 | Facebook Job Search Strategies

- Keep your page private to avoid prospective employers from seeing pictures meant for friends and family only.
- Is your Wall visible? Forty-five percent of employers are checking it out. Only post what you want them to see.
- Reconnect with former classmates, friends and colleagues; it just might help land you a job.
- Search corporate fan pages for job postings (e.g., Hyatt Hotels and Resorts).

Chapter 5.3 | Google and Your Job Search

- Yes—85% of hiring managers are Googling you.
- Set up a Google alert on yourself to monitor what Google has on you.

- Take action to correct and remove any inaccurate or false information appearing on Google, including images.
- Google results can cost you a job, even after the offer is extended.

Chapter 5.4 | Linking In to a powerful job search network

- Create a powerful, polished and results-filled profile on LinkedIn.com.
- Request recommendations from your contacts— gather a total of at least five.
- Get connected: groups, events and build your network.
- Take advantage: seek expert advice and ask questions.

Now that you're spending time online socializing for jobs, networking and connecting with other professionals, it's time to introduce which job boards are the best – not that you'll be using those to get a job. You already know that only 20% of jobs are found that way, right?

CHAPTER SIX

THE OTHER 20%

	9		6			3		
				8	3			5
2					7			
	8					5		
3				6			4	
	1							2
		7						
1			5		9		6	
		4		3		7		

"Look for an occupation that you like and you will not need to labor for a single day in your life."
- Confucius

As you learned in chapter four, 80% of jobs are found through networking, which is why I recommend you divide your blocks of time into an 80/20 split and only focus 20% of your time on the tactics in this chapter. To truly win the job search game, I recommend developing a game plan, so set aside time each day to do actual searching, whether it's 30 minutes or eight hours.

When you're out networking with a powerful 30-second pitch, the leads you'll be getting from new contacts and even standing in line at the coffee shop will be filling up the 80% part of your time. This chapter is focused on how to effectively use the other 20% of your time.

Chapter 6.1 | Developing Your Job Search Game Plan

On the next page is a worksheet you can use to develop your own job search game plan. Landing a new job is a big goal, right? It becomes much less daunting—and easier to accomplish—when you break it down into daily and then weekly activities.

Looking at this worksheet, you can track which tactics you're spending your time on and set out with a plan for the week ahead, knowing you're ready with a strategy. By the time Saturday comes around, you'll feel like you've conquered the world because you achieved your goals.

You spent 80% of your time networking, 20% on job boards, social networking and with recruiters. Your calendar will be booked with networking for the next week and your inbox is full of follow-up e-mails ready to send. Did you notice Sunday is missing from the game plan? Everyone deserves a day off. Choose the day you like best; I chose Sunday. *A relaxed, refreshed and rejuvenated mind is the best way to get positive results and win the job search game.*

Job Search Game Plan

Tactic	Monday	Tuesday	Wednesday	Thursday	Friday	Saturday
Face to Face Networking						
Thank You Notes (to Networking contacts)						
Reaching out to set up Networking Meetings						
Sending Resumes to Job Postings						
Online Searching						
Social Networking (twitter, facebook, LinkedIn®, etc)						
Job Boards						
Recruiter Calls						
Recruiter Meetings						
Email Follow-Ups (job boards)						
Total Hours, Job Searching:						
% of Time, Networking:						
% of Time, Other:						

If you find yourself out of balance with the 80/20 methodology, simply make an adjustment and you'll be on track to win the job search game the next day. Give yourself a break and realize these tools are to help you focus on the good you're doing and to see where you can improve your strategy.

Chapter 6.2 | Job Board Overload

Have you ever Googled "job boards"? Wow. It gives you about 25,800,000 results in 24 seconds. How are you as a job seeker expected to know what job boards are the best and where you're going to find the right jobs for you? There are the top three results, which are paid for and sponsored results, followed by the first 10 pages of listings for everything from diversity job boards to executive job boards to local job boards.

Just about every professional organization and social network offers a job board. Newsletters and alumni groups have job boards—and then there are the well-known job Websites like Monster.com. Today's competitive market has created job board overload.

It's important to note that when you're on a job board, you're being primarily searched *by* a recruiter. According to the *Wall Street Journal*, 73% of recruiters spend time online searching for candidates. Recruiters I've spoken with say they use LinkedIn.com for executive-level (director and above) candidates and give preference to those with recommendations.

Where's the action?

Competitive analysis is key to knowing where your fellow job seekers are searching for jobs. Why? The competition on these job boards is fierce.

According to a recent study by Greenfield Online, the following are job boards your fellow job seekers are hitting up most often:

- 61%: Monster.com
- 30%: Hotjobs.com
- 25%: Jobs.com
- 20%: Headhunter.com (bought by CareerBuilder.com)
- 15%: Career.yahoo.com

Applier Beware: Cons of Job Boards

Many postings on the major sites, as listed above, are from recruiters, headhunters and executive-search firms. When you post your résumé, you become a target for recruiters that may not have a job for you but will call you to source other names and numbers of co-workers who may be a fit for the recruiter's job listings. A recent candidate who worked in marketing included "marketing," "promotions," "advertising" and "events" as key terms on his job board posting. He started receiving promotions about highlighting (for a fee) his résumé in the advertising section and for job postings for insurance sales, cooks, camp counselors and other unrelated jobs.

One way to avoid this from happening is to apply for jobs directly on company career sites. More companies are listing their jobs on job sites and linking the job post back to their company career page.

Some job candidates set up alternative e-mail addresses for job board-related activity that can be easily deactivated after the job search is over. These e-mail addresses are great for filtering fee-based offerings that job boards are now sending to candidates.

Competition is the #1 con of job boards. Just because you find a job on a job board doesn't mean you have to apply for it on that job board. The best news is now you know the company has an opening. Take advantage of that knowledge and use the networking skills and tools you have from chapters four and five to get your foot in the door directly.

Find a person using the six degrees of connection concept and figure out who knows the hiring manager or corporate recruiter. Use LinkedIn to find someone in your network who works at the company and reach out to get the hiring manager's name. Worst-case scenario, call the company's main phone number, ask for the recruiting department and ask the receptionist to confirm that Donna Ivans is the hiring manager for that graphic design position you want. What's the worst that will happen? The person on the other end of the phone could say "no"—but he or she could also give you the correct name. The job search game just got easier.

Your last resort (always) is sending your résumé via the job board's posting information.

Chapter 6.3 | Top 30 Job Boards

Each year, WEDDLE's conducts a year-long ballot of recruiters and job seekers to determine which job boards rank best. The 30 sites that accumulate the most votes during the year are named WEDDLE's User's Choice Award Winners and they're coined as the "elite" of online employment sites.

This list shows what's occurring right now in today's competitive market. For example, technology-related job boards were popular just a few years ago, and today, there are only two on the list yet there are five health care-related job boards. A year from now, the categories will shift again. The job market is changing, and as a job seeker, you have to shift with it. Use this list to your advantage and focus first on job boards that specialize in your industry or profession.

The WEDDLE's Top 30 list is typically shown either alphabetically or in the order of their rank. To make your job search easier, I am giving you the top 30 job boards by category.

General Job Boards: All Careers
Monster: www.monster.com
Career Builder: www.careerbuilder.com
Direct Employers: www.directemployers.com
Diversity Jobs: www.diversityjobs.com
Employment Guide: www.employmentguide.com
GetTheJob: www.getthejob.com

Indeed: www.indeed.com

Job: www.job.com

JobFox: www.jobfox.com

Jobing: www.jobing.com

Simply Hired: www.simplyhired.com

SnagAJob: www.snagajob.com

Top USA Jobs: www.topusajobs.com

Yahoo Hot Jobs: www.hotjobs.com

Executives and $100K+ Job Boards

The Ladders: www.theladders.com

6FigureJobs:www.6figurejobs.com

ExecuNet: www.execunet.com

Recent College Grad Job Boards

AfterCollege: www.afterCollege.com

College Recruiter: www.collegerecruiter.com

College Grad: www.collegegrad.com

Tech Job Boards

Dice: www.dice.com

Jobs In Logistics: www.jobsinlogistics.com

Health Care Job Boards

Absolutely Health Care: www.absolutelyhealthcare.com

AllHealthcareJobs: www.allhealthcarejobs.com

HCareers: www.hcareers.com

Health Career Web: www.healthcareerweb.com

HealtheCareers Network: www.healthecareers.com

Vet Jobs: www.vetjobs.com

Retail
All Retail Jobs: www.allretailjobs.com

Temporary
Net Temps: www.net-temps.com
Sologig: www.sologig.com (not on WEDDLE's list; my own addition)

Many of these job boards have yet to integrate mobile or social capabilities despite the clear growth of apps on Apple's iPhones, iTouches and iPads and on BlackBerrys and Droids. Until job boards connect with users the way users communicate today, you'll have to continue to log in online to access the job postings and apply.

Chapter 6.4 | Recruiters, Search Firms and Headhunters

"73% of recruiters spend time online searching for candidates."

– Quintcareers.com

I remember being on the playground as a kid playing kickball. The first thing we had to do was pick teams. First the team captain was selected and then it came to everyone else. We stood there patiently thinking, "Pick me! Pick me!" I don't know about you, but for me, this process wasn't fun. By the time I was 12, I had a mouth full of braces, red-framed glasses (Hey, my mom said they looked good on me...), and despite my sunny disposition, I was no more attractive at that stage than most 12-year-old girls.

This is what it feels like for most job seekers when they're working with a recruiter, search firm or headhunter: vulnerable. "Pick me to present to your client." "I know I'll ace the interview." "I'm definitely the right person for the job." "They'll love me; just give me a chance!"

At the end of the day, the only person you get to talk to is a "screener" (aka recruiter, headhunter). It might feel like it was a waste of time, but was it? Let's look at what a recruiter does and what he or she can offer you in today's job search game.

1. Corporate recruiters: employed by a company for the purpose of finding and qualifying new employees for the organization. For this chapter, we'll focus on other types of recruiters as corporate recruiters are considered part of the company's HR department.

2. Contingency recruiters (aka headhunters): maintain a non-exclusive relationship with the company and are only paid a fee when a candidate they discovered is hired by the company. (The majority of recruiters fall into this category because it's free to the employer unless the recruiter finds them the right candidate.)

3. Retained recruiters (aka executive search or headhunter): focus on executive searches and get a retainer (up-front fee) to perform a specific search for a corporate officer or other senior executive position that typically pay upwards of $100,000.

Search fees are usually 33% of the annual compensation of the retained executive and the fee is for the time and expertise of the search firm. The firm is employed to conduct the entire recruitment effort, from sourcing the candidate until the candidate has started working.

Since the majority of recruiters are contingency recruiters, I'm going to give you advice on how to get the most out of the time you spend talking to and working with a contingency recruiter.

If you find yourself speaking with recruiters and then never hearing back from them or if you've sent out dozens (or hundreds) of résumés to recruiters only to get radio silence in return, don't get discouraged. This happens to plenty of job seekers. You're not alone.

These recruiters earn 20-30% or more of a candidate's first year's salary. If they sent over every résumé they got to the company, it would be bombarded. Keep in mind that the company is paying good money to have résumés and candidates heavily screened. It's in the recruiter's best interest to only send the cream of the crop.

Spot an Amateur

The first sign of an amateur contingency recruiter—or "fishermen," as I like to call them—is a recruiter who does nothing except collect résumés. If you're contacted by a recruiter and asked to send your résumé, *stop*. You're likely involved in a fishing expedition. To make sure, ask questions. After all, you don't want to ignore a real job opportunity.

These questions will help you filter fishermen recruiters:

- How did you get my name and contact information?
- Do you have a specific job in mind for me?
- What clients do you think my skills are a good match for?
- Once you have my résumé, when can I expect to hear from you next?
- Will you ever send my résumé to a client without my prior approval?

Spot a Professional

A professional recruiter only wants to work with candidates who fit his or her profile and who he or she considers to be a good candidate for the job and company. It's easy to spot these recruiters because they will ask you questions about your professional experience, education, results, etc.

Listen for these types of questions when talking to a recruiter:

- What are you looking for in a new employer/company?
- Would you consider relocating? If so, where?
  (Recruiters may push the legal envelope here and ask about a spouse and children to determine your likelihood to stay long-term at a job if you do relocate.)
- What type of position are you looking for next?
- Why did you leave your last company?

Professional recruiters want to do a good job for their clients (the company) and they want to keep your best interests in mind, too. If you become a satisfied candidate, you become one of their best sources of referrals. Professional recruiters are likely to treat you with respect and stay in communication with you, even if they don't have a job for you right away.

To increase your chance of success working with a recruiter, be clear, concise and confident about what you're looking for in a new position. They get passed job leads all the time, and if they know what your ideal job is and that you have the results to prove you can do the job, they'll be happy to refer you. Why? Because they'll make money just by placing you in that job, and if they already know you and have your résumé on hand, it'll be a fast hire.

Chapter Six | The Other 20% | Review

Chapter 6.1 | Job Search Game Plan
- Determine the amount of time each week to dedicate for job search.
- Divide your time: 80% to networking tactics and 20% to other tactics.
- Break down your activities into daily tasks, giving yourself a weekly sense of accomplishment.
- Give yourself a day off every week to refresh and rejuvenate.

Chapter 6.2 | Job Board Overload
- Use the top five most active sites: Monster.com, HotJobs.com, Jobs.com, Headhunter.com, Careers.yahoo.com.
- Know the #1 con of job boards: competition is fierce.
- Yes—73% of recruiters spend time online searching for candidates.
- Recruiters use LinkedIn.com to search for executive-level talent.

Chapter 6.3 | Top 30 Job Boards
- WEDDLE's Top 30 results include the five most active job boards.
- Pay attention to application instructions; apply directly on company career site, if applicable.
- Use networking tools from chapter four to apply for the job.

Chapter 6.4 | Recruiters, Search Firms and Headhunters

- Corporate recruiters work inside the company, are part of HR or are hired by the company.
- Contingency recruiters are paid a fee only when the candidate is hired
- Retained recruiters are paid a flat fee, are retained to do the entire search and focus on $100,000+ searches for executive-level talent.
- Spot an amateur or professional recruiter by asking or listening for the right questions.

Recruiters and Job Boards are a necessary part of the job search game, and a comprehensive strategy. That's why I've included this chapter, although it's important to remember these parts should only make up 20% of your strategy.

If you're thinking that applying to a job from a job board will land you the interview, or get you the job, because you're the most qualified, you've fallen for one of the Top 20 Job Search Myths. I'm going to debunk those myths for you so you can build your strategy based on facts, not myths.

CHAPTER SEVEN

TOP 20 JOB SEARCH MYTHS DEBUNKED

	9		6			3		
				8	3			5
2					7			
	8					5		
3				7			4	
	1							2
	7							
1		5		9		6		
	4		3		7			

"Shallow men believe in luck. Strong men believe in cause and effect.

- Ralph Waldo Emerson

Luck is a funny thing, isn't it? I prefer to think of the good things that happen to me as the effect of my efforts.

Without going into a philosophical discussion about the universe, law of attraction, karma or religion, I will simply say that regardless of what you believe in, I'm going to go out on a limb and say that life requires you to take some action (cause) in order to receive something (effect).

For argument's sake, I'm going to say that if you focus your energy on acing an interview and see yourself as confident, strong and motivated during the interview, then that's the experience you're going to have. In the same vein, if you're focused on job search myths, you're energy is going to go in the wrong direction.

Let's get these job search myths all cleared up and out of your way so you can stay on the track to winning the job search game. Here we go.

Chapter 7.1 | Top 5 Job Search Myths Debunked

Job Search Myth #1

Job searching during the summer or November/ December (the holiday season) is pointless. Companies don't hire during these times.

Someone tell the companies this and the recruiters, too. When I was a corporate executive and it came time to review my budget for the next year, I would hurry up and try to spend the rest of my budget in Q4, which meant that whoever I didn't hire during the rest of the year was about to get a call back with a job offer in November and December. I had money, and it needed to be spent. (Many executives spend up their budgets so they don't have them cut the next year.)

Companies also loosen the reins on hiring in the summer months because they have a stable pattern of earnings from Q1 and Q2. Their revenue patterns are solid enough to make hiring decisions without fear that their projections are unfounded.

Last, if you look at the time frames, they align more with when job seekers want to take vacations—summer and winter holidays. That's okay; however, think of it this way: with less job seekers in the competitive market because of this widespread myth, you have less competition.

Job Search Myth #2

Job boards are the best place to find a new opportunity.

People hire people. Unless something has changed dramatically, a computer is not hiring anyone. Then again, that iPad *is* something.

As demonstrated in chapter six, competition on these job boards is fierce...ferocious. How ferocious? More than 11 million people per month are logging onto Monster.com. No matter where in the U.S. or world you live, your competition for a job is never going to be 11.8 million people in one month. Job boards are simply just not the best place to find a new opportunity. They're the best place to find a new recruiter, given the 73% of them searching for candidates online.

The more you connect with people during your job search, the shorter your search will be and the better the job you land will be. Job board competition is oversaturated and you become a mere piece of paper rather than a face, a personality and someone with abundant skills.

Using your job search game plan and focusing on the ABC News report that 80% of jobs are found through networking, build a strategy that keeps your time split 80% on networking and only 20% on job boards and the like.

Job Search Myth #3

Investing in a professional résumé review is unnecessary.

As stated in chapter one, employers reject 90% of résumés they receive. So, statistically, your résumé is likely to get rejected. Ouch. The best thing to ensure you land in that wonderful 10% is to get a professional résumé review. Résumés that get results in today's competitive market are focused on results and accomplishments. You need to show the company what you can do for them.

Real-Life Testimonial

Marie reviewed a résumé recently for a Los Angeles-based candidate named Lou. After looking at it for approximately seven minutes, she knew his job titles and the dates of his employment. That's it. She had no idea what he did, if he managed people, budgets, or what exactly his job title even meant.

Lou's #1 frustration in the job search game? Lack of response from résumé submissions…no surprise there.

A professional résumé review will provide you with the expert advice, tools and resources you need to create a résumé that will grab the hiring manager's attention—up front and immediately.

The bottom line is that even highly qualified candidates will lose interviews if their résumés are less than stellar. Invest in a professional résumé review with quality career service providers and your results will soar.

Job Search Myth #4

Networking is for salespeople, not job seekers.

Thank goodness you told me. Here I am including an entire chapter on networking naturally and then another one on social networking! Can you also tell this myth to Twitter's #jobs, #jobsearch, #hiring, #resumes, #interview...? Okay, enough of my sarcasm. You get the picture.

If you want success in the job search game, you need to network. That's the case if you're an executive assistant, a manufacturing manager or a vice president of marketing. You're seven to 10 times more effective face-to-face, says Melissa Giovagnoli, CEO of Networlding. Don't let your networking anxiety keep you from landing a new job.

Job Search Myth #5

Phone interviews don't need thank-you notes.

Thank-you notes are never optional, even for phone interviews.

Ninety-five percent of phone interview candidates don't send a thank-you note, which means if you do you'll be at the top of the list. Interview thank-you note protocol is covered in chapter three; remember to send one to each person who interviews you. Personalize each note with something different. Include a piece of information you gathered during the interview to make a connection and to let the interviewer know you were listening. Recruiters count as interviews and deserve thank-you notes as well.

Chapter 7.2 | Top 10 Job Search Myths Debunked

Job search myths have been around for decades and while some of them come and go, others remain the same. The next set of job search myths begins with one that's rather new and needs to be debunked in today's economic climate.

Job Search Myth #6

It's not me, it's the economy.

There are no two ways around it: this economy is difficult and it's downright awful at times. That's why I wrote *Career Sudoku: 9 Ways to Win the Job Search Game*: to give you the tools, skills and resources to win the job search game in any economy.

There are jobs to be had. This is true or 11.8 million people wouldn't be spending time on Monster.com every month. The U.S. Department of Labor reported that unemployment benefits applications dropped for the third straight week in a row (May 2010). According to the U.S. Bureau of Labor Statistics, employers hired an average of 4.1 million workers per month between July and October, and there were 2.2 million additional job openings on the last day of October in 2009. Among the areas most likely to lead the hiring train in 2010 and beyond are health care, information technology, government and energy.

Challenger, Gray & Christmas, Inc., an outplacement firm, states that less than 20% of jobs are placed on job sites or ads. The bulk of hiring takes place in the "hidden" job market, where jobs are never advertised to the general public. Pull out your networking tools and hit the market hard to get these opportunities.

This economy is tough, no doubt about it and no denying it. There are jobs—at every level—so apply your new skills and perseverance with a strategic plan and you'll have one of them sooner rather than later.

Job Search Myth #7

Facebook doesn't affect my job search.

Tell that to Kate who was phone interviewed for a director-level position when the vice president on the other end mentioned Costa Rica and what looked to be a nice kayaking trip she had taken. Kate's heart sank immediately as images of her in a bikini standing in front of the bright yellow kayak flashed through her head. As you found out in chapter five, 45% of employers use Twitter and Facebook to screen job candidates. Make sure your Facebook page and Tweets are professional and only personal enough that you would be willing to share them with a potential employer.

If you want the freedom to be yourself in the realm of social networking, create an avatar identity. Plenty of job search candidates do this. This way, you can post anything you want without fear that it'll come back and bite you in the toukas. Twitter and Facebook also let you lock down your pages to a degree—privacy settings to protect your Tweets, limit your profile visibility, etc.—this is another option available to you.

Whatever you think about social networking sites, remember that with nearly half (and likely people more when you factor in recruiters) of all employers using social networking tools to screen you, it's a good idea to maintain a professional online appearance.

Job Search Myth #8

The most qualified candidate will get the job.

If only this really was the case! When you factor in that employers reject 90% of the résumés they receive and that nearly 85% of hiring managers only look at the top half of your résumé, the most qualified candidate may not even get an interview.

It's more likely that the candidate who lands the job is the seeker with the best combination of experience, education, personality and rapport with the interviewer...in short, *the most skilled interviewer* rather than the most qualified.

When you land an interview, you've passed step one and it means your skills, experience and education look to be a good match based on the employer's requirements for the job. Now it's up to you to sell them on *why* you're a good fit for the company (see chapter three).

Job Search Myth #9

Cover letters are optional.

This has become more than just a myth lately; it's become a modus operandi for some candidates. If this is you (I won't tell, I promise), now is a good time to change things up.

Cover letters are a must. No, e-mail is not a cover letter. Your cover letter is you saying, Hello, prospective employer. I'm the perfect person for you! It's an introduction to you, your résumé and what you can do for the company. Why skip it? See chapter one for catchy cover letters.

Job Search Myth #10

In tough times, take the first job offered.

This is a difficult myth to address for one reason alone: Is it a *good* job offer? If it is, go for it. Let me clarify.

Real-Life Testimonial

Brad wanted to work at The Artisan Group as a client relations director. Brad and I started working together and two weeks later he landed an interview. During the recruiting process, the company's recruiter told him that the position paid $10K less than what he wanted. My advice was to stay firm with his salary and to focus his efforts on a salary range.

Four days after the interview, the recruiter called to let him know he was their top candidate and she was confident they could meet his salary requirements. He got the job and started two weeks later.

In Brad's case, he took the first job offered because it was his ideal job at a great salary. If this is what you're facing, then by all means, go for it. Otherwise, focus on a job you want to take that meets your career goals and salary requirements. Realistically set your requirements and then go after your job search with an assertive, motivated and strategic plan.

Chapter 7.3 | Top 15 Job Search Myths Debunked

In a recent media interview, I was asked about advice job seekers request most often today compared to five years ago. The next job myth speaks directly to how I answered this question. Five years ago, the job search game was all about salary negotiations. Today it's about personal branding (as well as re-branding) and what it is, why it's necessary and how to do it.

Job Search Myth #11

Re-branding is for marketing people and products only.

Personal branding or re-branding is the difference between a job seeker and a successful job seeker. As you read in chapter two, a personal branding statement is a powerful 30-second pitch that answers "What do you do?" with an elegant combination of personal information, professional results and accomplishments, and wraps it all up with a statement about what you can offer a new company.

Starting with a UVP, you'll have a hook to answer this tough question in less than 15 seconds and in less than 15 words. When people ask who you are, respond with your hook. For example: "Hi, I'm Adriana, a *New York Times* best-selling author and speaker."

It immediately prompts the person you're speaking with to ask a follow-up question, such as "What's the name of your book?" or "What topic do you speak about?"

Why is branding yourself important? As actor Tom Cruise said in *Jerry Maguire*, "Help me help you." If I know what you do, I can help you.

When I ask what you do and your response is, "I'm the marketing director at AT&T," there's no reason for me to ask any other question or to continue the conversation. Alternatively, if your response is, "I'm a global marketing executive with a $50M budget at a leading Fortune 100 communications company," I will likely want to know more... what communications company, what countries do you work in, what type of marketing?

Personal branding: it's less a myth and more a job seeker's marketing tool for success.

Job Search Myth #12

Arriving late for an interview is okay as long as I call.

It's true that things happen in life that are unavoidable. Traffic, weather, babysitters canceling, etc., and all these can affect whether you show up on time to an interview.

Arriving late also affects whether you get the job or someone else gets the job. **Arriving late to an interview is**

never acceptable. If an emergency arises, you're better off rescheduling than showing up late. It sounds so cliché, but it's absolutely true: you only have one chance to make a first impression. Do you want to leave a hiring manager with the impression that you can't manage your time well?

Eight seconds. That's how long it takes to decide if the hiring manager is going to hire you. If you're not there in the first eight seconds, the choice is pretty easy! Give yourself every possible advantage you can and show up early—10 minutes early—and never late.

Job Search Myth #13

Don't take notes during an interview.

This myth makes sense to me. Interviews are filled with anxiety and nerves; you're trying to make sure you do everything just right because you want to get the job. What if taking notes makes you look bad—or worse, stupid?

First things first, taking notes makes you look smart, engaged and interested in the position, the company and the hiring manager. It's a compliment to the interviewer if you ask to take notes. Calm your fears with confidence. Since you're ready to impress with thoughtfully prepared questions for the interviewer, lift the first page of your legal pad on the right side of your pad folio and take notes on page two.

Insider Tip: Use notes you take during the interview to customize your thank-you note.

Job Search Myth #14

Spell-check will catch errors on my résumé.

Spell-check does catch some errors in a document, but not all of them. This has been the #1 résumé faux pas for the decade-plus that I've been a career coach and continues to be the top faux pas. The spell-check dilemma does not discriminate based on salary, position or profession. If you're a C-level executive or administrative professional, it's a smart move to triple spell-check your résumé prior to sending it out.

Don't forget about grammatical errors as well! Refer back to chapter one for the most common typos seen in business communications (including résumés, cover letters and e-mails to hiring managers). After you run spell-check, do a human check on your résumé and then ask a friend to check it again. Better yet, if you're able to, invest in the services of a professional copyeditor.

Job Search Myth #15

Changing jobs frequently is frowned upon by employers.

The "job hopper" mentality is passé, but you're more likely to run into a roadblock if you've been with your current employer for more than five years. This is a stark reality for many to face, as staying with an employer was once seen as being loyal. Just a few years ago, someone who stayed with his or her company was regarded as having a strong work ethic.

In today's competitive job market, you're seen as smart, savvy and assertive if you switch jobs every couple of years to capitalize on a new opportunity. Moving around allows you to keep up with industry changes, shifting work environments and changing climates.

Continuing to stay with one employer creates a more stagnant employee in some employer's minds, and that can lead to a less dynamic and creative candidate. This is most challenging for candidates who have the most experience (15+ years) in the workforce. Many of these candidates joined employers such as United Airlines, Nortel Networks, the Ma Bell Telecom companies and the like when there was a virtual "employment for life" sign over their heads. Although absolutely possible, it's difficult for a long-term employee to transfer his or her experience to another position—far more difficult than for a candidate who changes jobs frequently.

Note that if there's a consistent pattern of job changes every six to 12 months for the past three-plus years, employers will frown upon the candidate.

Chapter 7.4 | Top 20 Job Search Myths Debunked

I find it interesting that while researching for *Career Sudoku: 9 Ways to Win the Job Search Game*, few resources existed that addressed much more than the myths themselves. What good does it do you to know what the myth is if you don't know how to address it? The following five myths are researched in depth and then analyzed to ensure there's no factual basis to them.

Job Search Myth #16

I know how to answer interview questions or can figure it out when I get there.

Interview preparation is underrated and over-ignored when it needs to be hyper-focused on these days. With the hiring process taking 4.5-14.4 weeks, according to the 2009 EDGE Report conducted by Robert Half International and CareerBuilder.com, quite a bit of time elapses from the first interview to the offer letter.

The toughest interview question, "Tell me a little about yourself," often trips up the most confident interviewers. As you learned in chapter three, the best way to answer this is with your powerful 30-second pitch, which will get you off to a great start.

Figuring out the answers when you're already in the interview is too late. Remember that the best interviewer rather than the most qualified candidate gets the job and wins the job search game. Do a mock interview session with a friend or colleague. Better yet, hire a career coach and invest in an interview preparation session.

Job Search Myth #17

Lowering salary requirements makes me more attractive.

Confidence makes you look like a rock star. Assertiveness makes you eye-catching. Knowing your value makes you appealing. Lowering your salary requirements simply makes you *less valuable* rather than more attractive.

You're worth as much as you determine you're worth. Use tools such as salary.com and payscale.com to determine your market value based on your skills, education and years of experience. Then factor in your targeted industries and positions to determine the appropriate salary requirements and set realistic salary expectations.

Some candidates had inflated compensation packages in the late 1990s and early 2000s, and the economic climate of today will reset them to more realistic salary levels. The majority of Americans, however, have appropriate salary requirements that are in line with market values.

I recommend setting realistic, strong, confident salary requirements aligned with the market value of where you live, work and what your education and experience fits.

Job Search Myth #18

Sending out cover letters and résumés will get you interviews.

I just answered a question today from a follower on Twitter on why he wasn't getting response to his résumé and cover letter submissions. I Tweeted back: "Who are you sending them to? 80% of jobs are found through networking. Focus your efforts on those that will reap rewards."

If you send your résumé and cover letter to people you met in person through networking as a matter of follow-up, then this is less a myth and more a fact; you're likely to get interviews from these efforts. Alternatively, sending your résumés and cover letters out in response to job board postings or other job listings is going to net very few interviews, and most of the interviews you do land will be with recruiters.

Job Search Myth #19

Changing careers is nearly impossible.

Training director to global marketing communications manager—now that's a change of careers, yes? If you agree, then this is a myth for sure. It was me who made that career change at Level 3 Communications more than a decade ago, and they paid me to do it.

Changing careers is less a myth and more a reality for many professionals, particularly in today's changing economic climate. Now is a good time to move from one profession to another or to transfer to a new industry.

The health care industry is growing as the baby boomer generation ages. The eco-friendly movement has created the modern "green" industry that would have no employees if professionals never changed careers.

Grab your confidence, identify your transferrable, industry-agnostic skills and go for the career you've always wanted. You deserve it.

Job Search Myth #20

Telecommuting positions are just as productive.

While more companies in today's competitive market are moving toward this as a means to curb rising costs, telecommuting is still viewed as less productive and less efficient as in-office work. True or not, perception is reality in the business world, and this can cause quite an issue for telecommuting professionals. Why are they often passed over for promotions, raises and special projects? *Because they're less visible.* This lack of incentive and recognition contributes to low productivity levels.

One way to address this is to have regular face time in the physical office at your company.

Real-Life Testimonial

Jonathan, a telecommuting sales director based in Los Angeles, flew every six to eight weeks to his company's headquarters in Boston. This regular, face-to-face personal engagement with the 85+ people at Boston offices gave him a leg up on his other regional telecommuting counterparts throughout the country who did not put forth the same type of personal interaction.

When it came time for downsizing, Jonathan was kept on and his territory expanded. Was it his sales figures and quotas or his personal charm and engagement with the Boston team? One can only presume it was a combination of both his sales success and savvy personality.

Chapter Seven | Top 20 Job Search Myths Debunked | Review

Chapter 7.1 | Top 5 Job Search Myths Debunked

- Companies hire during summer and holiday season months.
- Job boards are not the best place to find a new opportunity.
- Investing in a professional résumé review is necessary.
- Networking is for job seekers.
- Phone interviews need thank-you notes.

Chapter 7.2 | Top 10 Job Search Myths Debunked

- Jobs exist, even in a tough economy.
- Facebook does affect your job search.
- The best interviewer gets the job.
- Cover letters are not optional.
- In tough times, don't necessarily take the first job offered.

Chapter 7.3 | Top 15 Job Search Myths Debunked

- People can be branded and re-branded.
- Arriving late for an interview is never acceptable.
- Take notes during an interview.
- Spell-check will not catch errors on your résumé.
- Changing jobs is considered smart.

Chapter 7.4 | Top 20 Job Search Myths Debunked

- Know how to answer interview questions ahead of time.
- Lowering salary requirements doesn't make you more attractive.

- Sending out cover letters and résumés won't always get you an interview.
- Changing careers is possible.
- Telecommuting positions are not as productive as in-office positions.

These myths were never anything you believed anyway, so now that you know they are, for sure, based on nothing, let's prepare you to negotiate the best job offer of your career.

CHAPTER EIGHT

JOB OFFER NEGOTIATIONS: WINNING THE GAME

	9		6			3		
				8	3			5
2				7				
	8					5		
3				8			4	
	1							2
		7						
1			5		9		6	
		4		3		7		

"You get more with sugar than you do with spice."
-Susan D. Klingenmaier

You'd be hard pressed to find me in a kitchen yet I live by this quote and am often found saying it to my clients. Why?

Because when it comes to negotiating a job offer and salary, the more sugar you use the more chance you have at winning the game.

Seventy-seven cents. That's how much women make for every $1 a man makes. Yes, it's 2010 and women still earn only 77 cents for every $1 a man earns. Minorities, and minority women in particular, face an even larger gap.

Compared to Caucasian men, African American women make 67 cents on the dollar (African American men make 78 cents); Hispanic women make about 58 cents (Hispanic men make almost 66 cents). Why consider the wage gap in a chapter about job offer negotiations?

Pay equity begins at the negotiation table. If you want to change pay equity and earn as much as your white male colleagues, then it starts with you. You control the negotiations and get what you deserve, and I'm here to give you the tools to do just that.

The same goes for white male professionals. The more you make, the higher the bar is for us to negotiate. Bring it on is the way I see it—competition is healthy and collaboration is even better.

Chapter 8.1 | Current Negotiation Landscape

Today's job market is fraught with fear and that fear leads job seekers to avoid salary negotiations as if they were the measles. Fear not. The current negotiation landscape is more open than you may think.

Sixty-one percent of employers surveyed said they're willing to negotiate a higher salary for qualified candidates (EDGE Report).

Why is now a better market to negotiate than when the economy was booming?

Employers have the pick of the litter, if you will, in today's job market, which means they're willing to pay a little more to get the right candidate. When a company has spent an average of three months recruiting and interviewing potential candidates for a position, it's an investment of time, money and resources on their end to find the "one" they want (aka *you*).

When they finally find you, it's as much a sense of relief and excitement for them as it is for you. They've likely searched through hundreds of résumés and cover letters, spent hours interviewing and now they're ready to offer you the job. You're the one they want, and many times they don't play all their cards up front.

Reverse Role Analogy

Today's housing market is a buyer's paradise. You have the pick of nearly any house you want and for a fraction of the price in some cases, given the high rate of foreclosures. You set a budget ($225,000) and call your realtor to find you the perfect house with four bedrooms and two and one-half baths. Weeks pass and your family looks at what feels like 500 listings your realtor has sent via e-mail.

A month later, you find four homes your family agrees you all want to see. You view all four and narrow it down to two final ones. After going back twice to each of the final two, you all agree that the one with the big backyard is it. It has everything you want: four bedrooms and two and one-half baths plus a den, and the kitchen was just remodeled exactly how you would have done it. The asking price is $230,000; it's out of your price range, so you offer $215,000 and hope for the best, knowing you're willing to go to $225,000 because this is the "one" you truly want.

The sellers need your offer and want to take it. They also need $222,000 to pay off their mortgage. They don't want to lose your offer yet are afraid to counter-offer since it's the only offer they've had in eight months.

In this housing analogy, you had leverage; you knew you could increase your offer and stay within your pre-determined budget of $225,000. The sellers, being in a more needy position, felt pressure to accept a lower offer.

Employers are using their recruiters like realtors in today's job offer negotiations. They're working to get the best candidate at the best price. It's your job to get the best offer possible and take care of your needs before day one.

Integrating market facts and factors and keeping results-based negotiations free of emotion and personal issues will get you closer to what you want.

Let's look at tactics to help you win the job offer negotiations game.

Chapter 8.2 | Winning Negotiation Tactics

1. Do your research.

Know what salary to expect for the position. Use resources such as salary.com and payscale.com.

2. Delay salary talks.

Hold off salary negotiations as long as possible. Ensure you understand everything the position entails prior to talking numbers.

3. Always let them go first.

Avoid being the first to discuss salary in any way, and refrain from being the first to give a number of any kind as well. If they ask what salary you expect, you say competitive with market value or provide a salary range.

4. Demonstrate you value.

It's always easier to pay more when you know you're getting great value. Demonstrate the value you're giving the employer. Know your strengths, achievements and be prepared to communicate them.

5. Inflation is a no-no.

Never inflate your current earnings to get a higher salary. It doesn't work and you could get the pink slip for it.

6. It's okay to say "no."

Don't feel obligated to accept the first offer unless it's what you want, of course. This is when you want to negotiate to reach a reasonable offer.

7. Smile.

Remember the phone interview tip to smile over the phone? The same applies here. Smiling during the negotiation process sends a friendly tone, which helps you get more of what you want.

8. Kill 'em with kindness.

Aggression never works in salary negotiations and can actually lead to an offer being withdrawn. Focus on being friendly and even-keeled during the negotiation process.

9. Use your personality.

Your personality, along with your skills and experience, landed the offer. Use it in the negotiation.

Men often negotiate better than women because they know how to use their personality to their advance. Ladies, use your talents during this process.

10. Think big.

Focus on more than just salary. Think about the entire compensation package (benefits, 401K, time off, etc.). Make the negotiation about more than just one number.

11. Go for more than money.

Look for other concessions (better title, office rather than cubicle, more vacation days, shorter review time, bonuses, etc.) that can offset a lower salary.

12. Develop options.

Create two or three options to respond with when you get into the negotiation process. Giving the employer more than one option allows them to feel they have power and choice. Make sure each option has what you want imbedded in it.

13. Let them win.

It's important for your new employer to feel like they've won the negotiation. To achieve this, include at least one item in each option that you know they will say "no" to, thereby giving them a sense of "winning" and creating a feeling that they have to give in to something else.

14. Role-play.

Negotiations are nerve-racking for many people. If you're one of them, role-play the negotiation with a friend, spouse or family member to calm your nerves and prepare for the actual event.

15. Understand your opponent.

All game players, from golfer Phil Mickelson to business titan Donald Trump, will tell you that in order to win it's essential you understand who you're playing against. You'll know the hiring manager from the interview, but you may be negotiating with the recruiter. Know your opponent in the negotiation to create a savvy negotiation strategy.

16. Know your minimum.

Everyone has a minimum salary and compensation package that's acceptable. **Before you head to the negotiations table, know your minimum acceptable offer level.** Are you okay with accepting X or do you really want Y in order to do this position?

If you want Y, then hold out for it because taking X may create workplace resentment on day 10, and that's no fun for anyone. On the flipside, if accepting X is great for you and they offer X off the bat, think twice before negotiating too hard.

17. Get it in writing.

It's never final until you have it in writing. Review the entire offer letter with a fine-tooth comb and check all the details. You may even want to send it to an attorney for review.

18. Take your time.

Most employers provide a five-day period for you to review and sign the offer letter. Don't feel rushed to sign it too quickly or respond right away. Give yourself a night to sleep on it and make sure you have the offer you want before you say "yes." If it's a verbal offer, tell them you'd like 24-48 hours to sleep on it and ask if they can send it to you in writing while you think it over.

Chapter 8.3 | 3 Ways to Successfully Negotiate the Best Job Offer

You have winning techniques for how to negotiate a great job offer; now it's time to give you three ways to successfully negotiate the actual offer. If you have to skim this chapter, read only this next part.

1st Way to Successfully Negotiate the Best Job Offer
➡ Know Your Value

Do you really know what your value in the market, to this company, in this position?

Real-Life Testimonial

I spoke with a candidate named Rachel recently. Based in Atlanta, Rachel was making $85,000 in a sales position working from home. She wanted to land a new job working outside her home, in an office environment. Her job search resulted in an offer for a marketing position at a major beverage company in Atlanta.

When she began interviewing, they told her the salary range for the position was $65,000-$72,000. Although she didn't want to take a reduction in pay, she was willing to do so in order to work with the company and meet her other job needs (e.g., work at an office, etc.).

Working together, Rachel and I researched the following components to prepare her for a successful job offer negotiation:

- Company information:
    o Number of employees
    o Annual revenues
    o Industry
    o Location (geography/region)

- Rachel's information:
    o Skills
    o Length of experience
    o Education
    o Management responsibility
    o Salary history

- Industry information:
    o Market value, position-specific
    o Average salary, position-specific
    o High and low salary, position-specific

2nd Way to Successfully Negotiate the Best Job Offer
➡ **Keep Your Number to Yourself**

You know the "don't ask, don't tell" policy? In job offer negotiations, it's more of a "do ask, don't tell" policy. Do what you can to get the company to show its hand and tell you what the pay scale, budget, salary range (call it what you will, just get them to tell you it) is before you share your salary requirements.

If you have to share a number first (it happens approximately 45% of the time) use these tactics to keep it a successful negotiation for you:

1. Provide a broad range based on your research.

2. Say "I expect a total compensation that's based on my unique set of skills and...(play to your strengths and demonstrate value).

3. Turn the question on them: "What does your market data show the position is worth?"

4. "Based on my unique set of skills, experience and research on market trends, I expect a fair overall compensation package. Is there a particular budget set for this position?"

Avoid, like the measles, sharing a specific number (e.g., "I'm currently making $68,300 and would like to stay in that range." or "I was making $103,000 in my last position, so I'd like to be in the $100,000-$110,000 range.")

3rd Way to Successfully Negotiate the Best Job Offer
➡️ **Prepare Counteroffers**

This is my favorite part of the negotiation process. Call me a little devilish, but I love (as in the big-bear-hug-yummy kind of love) when career coaching clients I work with get sweet-as-sugar job offers that make them smile from ear to ear. There's no better feeling in the world.

The key to getting a sweet job offer is preparing one heck of a counteroffer. All your counteroffers need to vary somewhat and can include more than just base pay.

Examples of what to include in a counteroffer:

- Base pay adjustment
- Bonuses
  - Performance-based
  - Quarterly
  - After 90 days
  - Annual
- Review time frame
  - 90 days
  - 60 months
  - 1 year
- Vacation time
- Stock options
- Flexible work schedule
- Benefit co-pays

I'm going to tell you up front that this is one of the primary areas that I differ from other career coaches. I say you prepare two or three counteroffers rather than just one, and I'm going to share with you why:

Reason #1 to prepare multiple job offer counteroffers:

Nearly 50% of all job seekers accept the first offer that's put on the table, compared to 61% of employers that are willing to negotiate a higher salary for qualified candidates.

Reason #2 to prepare multiple job offer counteroffers:

People like options and they like being in control even more. Giving your new manager options is great, giving him or her control is better. Give your new manager the "control" to decide what he or she wants to give you, and you're starting off on a great foot even before day one. (Hint: Every counteroffer has what you want so you win all around.)

Reason #3 to prepare multiple job offer counteroffers:

I've worked through hundreds of counteroffers, including a dozen of my own, and 95% of my clients get what they want 100% of the time. That's nearly triple the industry average (38%), and it's worked so well that my mailbox is my favorite place. Why? Because clients send me handwritten thank-you notes (I love these) and gift cards. Insane, right? They send me thank-you notes and gift cards after paying me to give them advice.

Enough reasons. Let's just do this so you can prepare your counteroffers, get the job offer you really want and win the job search game.

Chapter 8.4 | Successful Job Offer Negotiation in Action

With all these negotiation tactics, tips and techniques, what does it look like to put it into action and have it work? Let's take a look at a real-world successful job offer negotiation scenario.

Real-World Scenario

<u>Candidate</u>: Phil Davidlan

<u>Current Position</u>: senior marketing director; manages seven people; salary: $84,500/year

<u>Bio</u>: 8 years of experience in marketing; BA, communications

<u>Ideal Job Offer</u>: marketing executive position earning $88,000/year; working two days/week from home; would like to keep current three weeks of vacation

<u>Position Interviewed For</u>: marketing director

<u>Company</u>: Cates, a growth-oriented media company; $150M annual revenues; 100 employees

<u>Initial Offer</u>: Marketing director title; salary: $85,700/year; two weeks vacation; 100% paid benefits for him and his family

Counteroffer Option #1:

- Phil accepts the originally offered $85,700 salary
- Requests telecommuting two days/week from home
- Requests one additional week of vacation (aligning with his current three weeks)
- Title upgrade to senior marketing director (his current title)

(Most likely to get the vacation and title—zero cost to the employer's bottom line; the telecommuting is a good "no" option for the employer)

Counteroffer Option #2:

- Phil asks for increased salary to $86,850 (median of his ideal and their offer)
- Requests one additional week of vacation (aligning with his current three weeks)
- Title upgrade to senior marketing director (his current title)

(Most likely to get the vacation and title—zero cost to the employer's bottom line; he gets two "yes" items and they can say "no" to the salary increase)

Counteroffer Option #3:

- Phil accepts initial offer of $85,700
- Asks for a 90-day appraisal with salary increase up to $88,000
- Requests one additional week of vacation (aligning with his current three weeks)
- Requests telecommuting two days/week to work from home

(Most likely to get the 90-day appraisal and vacation— no risk or cost to the employer; he gets two "yes" items and they can say "no" to the telecommuting item)

Considerations:

(a) The company-paid benefits save Phil $350/month, adding $3,600/year to his salary. At the initial offer of $85,700 he's already ahead of the game, making $89,300 total compensation.

(b) At a senior marketing executive level, the company may have Phil managing a team, so working from home may not be viable. Therefore, this may be the easy "no" for the company.

(c) It's a good idea to include at least one counteroffer that accepts their original salary. If their initial offer and your desired salary are far apart, this may not be possible; however, if you're reasonably close—as is the case with Phil's scenario—give a way to let the employer win with their original offer.

It typically takes more than one phone call to negotiate the ideal job offer. Remember to remain friendly, calm and composed during the negotiation process. Employers want non-emotional new hires, and your personality during the negotiation process is just as important as it was during the interview process.

If an employer calls to negotiate and you're in a crowded coffee shop where you'll have difficulty hearing or speaking freely and talking openly, simply answer the call outside and explain that you're in a public place. Ask if you can call back at 2 p.m. that afternoon (or a time that's convenient for you to be in a quiet location where you will have a pen, paper and your counteroffer notes).

Chapter Eight | Job Offer Negotiations | Review

Chapter 8.1 | Current Negotiation Landscape

- Yes—61% of employers will negotiate a higher salary for qualified candidates.
- Recruiters have become realtors, shopping for the best candidate at the best price possible.

Chapter 8.2 | Winning Negotiation Tactics

- Do your research, delay salary talks, let them go first.
- Demonstrate value, inflation is a no-no, it's okay to say "no," smile.
- Kill 'em with kindness, think big, use your personality, and go for more than money.
- Develop options, let them win, understand your opponent, know your minimum.
- Get it in writing and take your time.

Chapter 8.3 | 3 Ways to Successfully Negotiate the Best Job Offer

- Know your value.
  - Research the company, industry, market and your skills to gather necessary information to determine the best salary you can negotiate for the position.
- Keep your number to yourself.
  - Your goal is always to get and never give a number first.
- Always prepare counteroffers.
  - Two is better than one; three is better than two. Be prepared with a few counteroffers so you have options.

o Include one item in each counteroffer that's an easy win for the employer.

Chapter 8.4 | Successful Job Offer Negotiation in Action

- Consider all options—cash, non-cash, salary, benefits and more.

You've done it, you landed the job and it's time to start day one at your new company. Enter the butterflies, again. What do you wear? How do you prepare? Do you take the long lunch with your co workers even though you're trying to make a good impression?

Relax. I'm still here with you. Let's walk through your first 90 days together *and* how to ace your 90 day performance appraisal.

CHAPTER NINE

AFTER YOU LAND: THE FIRST 90 DAYS

	9		6			3		
				8	3			5
2					7			
	8			9		5		
3						4		
	1							2
		7						
1			5		9		6	
		4		3		7		

"When your work speaks for itself, don't interrupt."
—Henry J. Kaiser

Woohoo! You did it! You won the job search game, from creating a résumé that got you the right result, to developing a great personal brand and powerful 30-second pitch, to landing the right interview and impressing the hiring manager, to negotiating your ideal job compensation package.

Now it's time to start the job, right? Beep. Beep. Beep. (Picture a big moving truck backing up since you can't hear me saying the beeps in person.) It's time to celebrate. Relax. Enjoy the moment. You've been working hard and you deserve to enjoy it a bit, don't you think? Break out some Kool & the Gang and "Celebrate." Oh, yeah, you know what I'm talking about...

"Yahoo! This is your celebration,

Celebrate good times, come on! (Let's celebrate),
Celebrate good times, come on! (Let's celebrate)

There's a party goin' on right here
A celebration to last throughout the years
So bring your good times, and your laughter too
We gonna celebrate your party with you"

*All lyrics are property and copyright of their owners and for educational purposes only.

Chapter 9.1. | Before Day One

You've landed a new job. What hasn't landed is the deposit in your bank account. I know the feeling. I may be an author, but it takes a while for the royalties to land into the bank account. And I know all too well how macaroni and cheese tastes three nights in a row. (Actually, I like to change it up with a bowl of multigrain Cheerios.)

It's important to celebrate your huge win one way or another. Whether your bank balance is $10,000, $100 or -$100 doesn't matter; what matters is that you give yourself permission to reward yourself for winning the job search game. Following are some creative ways, courtesy of successful job seekers, to celebrate landing a new job:

- See a movie in the park (many cities offer free screenings in the spring/summer).
- Take a weekend off from housework and go hiking with your dog.
- Meet a friend for a glass of wine.
- Splurge on a manicure or pedicure.
- Go for an extra-long walk with your favorite iPod tunes—barefoot on the beach.
- Buy a new pair of flip-flops ($3.50 at Old Navy).
- Buy a new white T-shirt.
  - o There's something nice about a fresh, crisp, white tee.
- Have dinner with a good friend.
- Get away for the weekend.
- Ask a friend to cook you a "congratulations" dinner.

- o You'll bring the wine, Perrier or dessert.
- Buy bubbles and take a bath.
- Get your favorite Dairy Queen treat.
- Enjoy a spa day with a girlfriend.
  - o At a spa.
  - o At home.
    - Homemade facial masks
    - Give each other mani/pedis
    - Sugar lip scrub
- Create a "vision board."
  - o Cut out pictures of what you want using magazines and catalogs.
  - o Paste them to a white poster board.
  - o Hang it in a visible place in your home.

Use your creative mind to come up with your own version of celebrating your hard-won success and have at it. The main concept is merely that you celebrate and whatever that means to you is wonderful.

After you've patted your own back, it's time to focus on how to keep the job you worked so hard to get.

The week before day 1

Test-drive your new route to work (or the train station, bus stop) to get comfortable with the commute. You might even want to leave at the same time in the morning that you need to when you start working to get a feel for the traffic patterns.

Eat well, sleep well, exercise, do anything you can to keep your energy level up going in.

Two nights before day 1

Go to bed early tonight, the same time you would if tomorrow was day one. If you're like most people, tonight is a Saturday night since you're starting work on a Monday. You want to stay up late; it's Saturday night so your body wants to stay up tonight and sleep in tomorrow. Go to bed early tonight and get up early tomorrow. You will be grateful come Monday morning.

The night before day 1

Pick out what you're wearing tomorrow and set it aside. Remember to include everything from your skivvies to your socks. (Oh, yeah, I said skivvies.) The last thing you want on the first day of your new job is to be running around the house looking for fresh skivvies.

Next up, set the alarms. If you usually use one alarm, set two. If you usually use two, set three. One alarm isn't enough: electricity goes out, alarms malfunction, batteries run low, you set the alarm for 7 p.m. instead of 7 a.m.—yes, it happens all the time. Tomorrow is the first day of a whole new journey for you, and you want to be sure you're up on time.

Wash your face, lay your head on a fresh pillow and hit the sack, Jack. Get a good night's rest.

Insider Tip: Avoid sleep aids before day one of your new job. Ambien, Tylenol PM and all the other cute "I can help you sleep" little sheep-counting helpers will have the *opposite* effect tomorrow. The first day of a new job is exhausting enough without that sleep-aid groggy feeling.

Chapter 9.2 | "Freshman Year" aka The First 30 Days

Do you remember your first day of high school as a new freshman? That's how many people feel the first day of a new job. By the end of The First 30 Days, that whole Freshman Year experience will be over, I promise.

Imagine if during your freshman year you had eaten properly, slept well and exercised so your energy was up and you felt great.

Go into your first 30 days and eat well, sleep well and exercise to keep up your energy. You're going to need it for the next 30 days. **According to self-improvement expert Steve Atchison, it takes 21 days to develop a habit.** In other words, your new routine is going to take some getting used to. The next month of your new job is going to be strenuous on your mind and body alike. Let's dig in to make it the most successful 30 days possible, shall we?

Day One Success Tips

- Arrive 10 minutes earlier than your scheduled start time.
- Bring protein-filled snacks (protein bars are convenient).
  - Protein keeps you feeling fuller longer.
  - Day one is usually packed with new hire-related paperwork; lunch might be late and you need your energy today.

- Grab your coffee ahead of arriving.
- Ask for what you need, when you need it.
    - o Being a new hire and a kidnapping victim are different. If you need a break, simply ask.
- Expect to be tired. It's normal.
- Google lunch places in advance, in the event you end up going alone (it happens).

<u>Days 2-30</u>

Now that you're no longer the new kid on the block, you'll be getting into the routine and settled into your position. Remember those 21 days to develop a habit? It'll start setting in during this period: waking up, getting dressed, driving to work (or taking the train, bus, etc.), working all day and heading home. This routine will become your new habit.

Go easy on yourself if you find that you're overly exhausted the first month of your new job; most people have this type of physical response. It may take up to 30 days for you to acclimate to your new schedule.

Remember the advice from the week before day one to eat well, sleep well, exercise, and do anything you can to keep your energy level up going in? The same advice applies during this time period. This is a physically grueling time as much as it's a mentally grueling time, and keeping yourself in good shape physically is imperative.

Get a Mentor

One of the best ways to start off at a new company is to get a mentor right away. Always look upwards for a mentor and find someone within the organization who's highly respected and in a position of authority. Quickly identify the people who can help you and figure out how to get in front of them. It's smart to identify two or three people you'd like as mentors in the event one of them is unable to take on the task.

Real-Life Testimonial

Leah started at a company and was hoping to have Kevin, the senior vice president of strategy, mentor her, given his reputation in the company, education and industry expertise. Her goal was to rapidly advance within the organization, and she knew he would be a great ally within the company. She could learn a great deal from him and help her move back into a global role, which she had experience with at a previous company.

Leah approached Kevin to be her mentor and he agreed, even mentioning that the idea had crossed his mind, as he was impressed with her. They set their first meeting for three weeks from then.

News of their mentoring relationship quickly spread throughout the company and people began seeing Leah differently. She was getting more respect because Kevin chose to mentor her. She liked it and knew she made a good choice.

The day of their first mentoring session came and went. He was called to London. This happened every time they were to meet, with one exception, for five months. Leah saw a successful executive in Kevin; however, he was a poor choice for a mentor.

Start Strong

Hit the ground running by playing to your strengths. You already know where you can make an immediate impact and that's what you want to focus on in the first 30 days with the company. What projects can you work on where your strengths will be highlighted?

Show Results

During the negotiation process, you focused on demonstrating your value and now it's about showing your results. Focus on what you can prove quickly without overpromising and underdelivering. Do you think you can sell $10,000 in the first 30 days? Great, say it and show them you can do it. It's better to do that than to say you can sell $250,000 and only deliver $10,000 in results.

On Time, All The Time

It's surprising how often people show up late for work, even in the first 30 days. Be on time every day—especially for the first 90 days. In the first 30 days, arrive early every day. This is a time to learn about your position and about the company, which means you can spend those extra 10 minutes when you arrive early learning all you can (and impressing the boss).

Be Observant

Your first 30 days is when the company, your new boss and the staff are observing you to get a feel for who you are and what your personality offers the company. This is a great time for you to be semi-transparent and observe how office politics play out, who the players in the company are and who the water cooler gossip group members are as well. Observe everything you can from a distance because you will soon be a deeply engaged member of the inner circle at the company.

Set Goals

During the interview you may have asked what goals and objectives you were responsible for meeting in your new position. Now is the time to clearly define these goals. The first 30 days can pass quickly without realizing that another 60 days later, you'll be face-to-face with your manager in a

90-day appraisal discussing your performance against these goals.

Let your manager know you C.A.R.E. about setting your goals and achieving them.

C = Clearly defined
A = Actionable
R = Results-focused
E = Easy to measure

Chapter 9.3 | "The Comfort Zone" Days 31-90

Now is when you become a part of the company culture and begin to find your place within the landscape. I call this "the comfort zone" because you have become just comfortable enough to let down your guard and let your personality shine through your new-hire anxiety.

After a month on the job, your body has acclimated to the routine and you have relaxed into the daily customs. You know that setting your alarm for 6:15 a.m. gives you enough time to get out the door by 7:23 a.m., which is precisely the time your stove clock must read for you to be at work and at your desk by 7:54 a.m.

Smart Scheduling

Something that may be moderately flexible, such as your schedule, is based on office cultural norms. By this point, you've had time to observe that, for example, your new office runs on a more relaxed schedule.

If you're there before the clock strikes 8:10 a.m., you look like a superstar and people think you've been there since 7:30 a.m. Everyone tends to leave between 4:30 p.m. and 5:15 p.m. You decide to leave around 5:20 p.m. with senior management to create an impression that you have a strong work ethic yet you also value work-life balance. You have this place figured out—or do you?

Beware of the comfort zone.

Making a good impression is just that, a good impression. While your impression is essential when starting at a new company, it's also your work that's being evaluated during the initial 90-day appraisal period. Remember: when you arrive early and stay late, engage in productive and results-focused work.

If you get there at 7:54 a.m., leave at 5:20 p.m. and are playing Farmville on Facebook, posting personal Tweets or doing your makeup in the bathroom, then why waste your time?

Real-Life Testimonial

Margaret was hired as a training coordinator and started out like a superstar, quickly becoming one of the leading employees in the department. After the first 30 days, yet still during the initial 90-day appraisal period, her manager began to notice that Margaret was arriving at work and then disappearing for 20 minutes shortly after her arrival.

This behavior went on for nearly a week when Margaret's manager picked up on what was going on. Margaret would arrive at work, log in to her computer and e-mail and then head to the bathroom to put on her makeup and do her hair.

The behavior exhibited by Margaret is unacceptable at any time. During the initial 90 days, your performance, behavior, actions and communications are under extra-close scrutiny because you're the new kid on the block. This is one of the reasons why the comfort zone can also be a danger zone. Following are suggestions for what to do with your time before/after other staff arrives:

1. Catch up on company research.
2. Prepare questions for colleagues and/or your manager.
3. Ask your mentor if he or she is available to have coffee at 7:45 a.m. before the day gets busy.

Lunchtime Trap

The first 90 days are exhausting both mentally and physically. When lunchtime rolls around, your mind and your body are ready for a break and need some refueling. If it's summer, you probably want a nice walk, fresh air and lunch. You probably even have some new friends and definitely some new colleagues you want to enjoy lunch with as well. So do I. Unfortunately for me and you on most days, our schedules don't allow for an hour and a half in the middle of the day to enjoy lingering business lunches.

What do you do? I have some great options for you.

First, if you've never heard of Yelp.com, it's all about "Real people. Real reviews." (That's their tagline, not mine.)

Yelp can become a lunchtime wonderland if you want it to be; opening doors to new restaurants that offer a variety of take-out, delivery and dine-in options all over the country. You might just look like the restaurant guru in the office; no one needs to know your secret.

Yelp in Action

I searched "business lunch" in "Chicago, 60610." Here's one of the top three listings:

Review #1 - Leisurely Lunch

Restaurant location: Michigan Ave. and Chicago

"Was here for lunch. Great service and an amazing burger! I love the 'we're all so busy, yet all seem to be busy doing nothing vibe'...very NYC."

I frequent this restaurant, although I've never been there for lunch. This review ensures I'll never go either since, like you, my schedule is busy doing something rather than nothing.

Review #2 - Normal Business Lunch

Restaurant location: Michigan Ave. and Chicago (same location)

"EVERY DAY! Everything you need to pick up for lunch or for your co-worker's lunches is right here. Smoothies are way better than Jamba right next door and Intelligentsia coffee."

This review excited me. I've never heard of this place, but you can bet I'll be heading there this week to check it out. (I can dig another brand of coffee over my usual Starbucks…)

It feels great to make friends with colleagues at your new company. They've worked there longer, which means they may be accustomed to taking hour-long lunches or special Friday hour-and-a-half lunches. Friends or not, these folks have little to prove if they've been there for years. Your position in the company, your value and results are still unproven, which means taking hour-long lunches in the first 90 days needs to be reserved for special occasions only.

- Is it your boss's birthday?
- Is your team celebrating a project success?
- Was a new team member hired and the whole group is going to lunch?
- Are you having lunch with your senior management mentor?

Last, make dining in a pleasurable option. Get away from that desk and your work! Grab a book, magazine or a notepad and enjoy your delivered, picked-up or homemade lunch. Eat it outside, in the office lunchroom or even in an empty conference room. Give yourself a break for 30 minutes; just avoid the long lunch times.

Dress to Impress

Here's one of the best pieces of advice I ever received in my career: **dress for the job you want, not the job you have.** At age 18, I was a title clerk making $9/hour at ORIX Credit Alliance. Where? By 21, I was senior manager of training and development with a $13M budget at what is now Qwest. I was responsible for the training curriculum of 4,000+ sales professionals in 14 states and was positioned to be global vice president within five years.

Whether you're a title clerk, a senior manager or global vice president, dress for the job you want instead of the job you have, even if you just landed it. SCORE reports that 65% of small businesses have casual office environments. Considering that small businesses represent 99.7% of all employer firms, there's a good chance you're working in an office with a casual dress code.

If you landed a new job in a Fortune 500 or other big business, you may still need to navigate the casual dress code waters on casual Fridays.

Here are five tips for successful casual dress:

1. **Jeans**
   a. Dark denim or white (women only)
   b. No holes, tears, rips or jagged marks
   c. Waistline should cover the top of your skivvies (I said it again.)

2. **Shoes**
   a. Polished
   b. Professional
   c. Heels or dressy flats (women)
   d. Casual dress shoes (men)
   e. No gym shoes, unless you work in a gym
   f. No designer athletic shoes (e.g., Puma, Chuck Taylors, Converse, Prada)

3. **Shirt**

   a. Cover your entire top half
   b. Button-downs always win
   c. Sex appeal is for after work
   d. Designer tops are a great way to integrate style
   e. Integrate color

4. **Blazer/Sweater**
   a. Great addition to step up a casual outfit
   b. Makes it easy to include you on higher-level meetings
   c. Immediately dresses up casual clothing
   d. Versatile look
   e. Keeps you warm in air-conditioned offices
   f. Easy to put on/take off when needed
   g. Adds level of sophistication to your look and impression

5. **Accessories**
   a. Great way to enhance a basic outfit
   b. Pair trendy fashion accessories with timeless clothes (saving tip)
   c. Chunky and heavy is okay
   d. Pearls always add elegance and intelligence to a look (women)
   e. Classic watch adds level of confidence and class (men)

You're arriving early, staying late, eating lunch with colleagues (yet not spending an hour and a half doing it), and dressing to impress. What could you possibly have left to do? There's one last thing: the 90-day appraisal.

Insider Tip: If you don't have a performance appraisal scheduled, request one. It shows initiative and that you're focused on results.

Chapter 9.4 | The 90-Day Performance Appraisal

If it feels like interview time again with butterflies in your belly and anxiety running from your fingers to your toes, you're completely normal. **The best way to relax prior to your performance appraisal is preparation.** Being prepared includes knowing what to expect.

Before anticipating those dreaded "things to improve upon" notes (which are never fun to hear but we do need to hear them), think of this process as a way for you to step up your game and bolster your overall package of abilities. *Feedback is valuable because it helps you perform better.*

Every organization differs in how they conduct appraisals. In the dot-com era, some companies began giving appraisals in open cubicles where other employees could hear the entire appraisal. While this was in the spirit of open communication and transparency, it was insensitive to the employee receiving the appraisal. Other organizations utilize 360-degree appraisals that start weeks prior to the actual employee and manager meeting. Evaluation forms are sent to the employee's peers, managers and, if applicable, subordinates to get a comprehensive view of the employee's performance. Although lengthy, this has become widely adapted in both large and small companies alike for the variety of feedback gathered during the process.

Performance Appraisal Preparation

1. Performance Appraisal Length

Appraisals vary in length from 30 minutes to an hour. Be ready to engage in a conversation with your manager. This may include reviewing your manager's comments, either in advance or during the meeting. Sometimes you will be asked to provide your comments, either in advance or during the meeting.

2. Review of Goals

In your first 30 days, your goals were set with C.A.R.E. This method pays off big during your first and subsequent performance appraisals. When clear goals are set at the beginning of a new position, your performance appraisal experience should be positive.

3. The Good, The Bad (and the Ugly)

As a career coach, I give clients insight, motivation, focus…and the 20% of the truth their friends and family hold back—the stuff (aka the ugly) people don't want to tell you because they're afraid it'll hurt your feelings.

During your performance appraisal, you want to be prepared for a similar experience. You should expect recognition for your accomplishments and discussion around areas that you can be improved upon.

4. Open Dialogue

Expect an open, honest and sincere dialogue about your performance. The dialogue should provide specific examples and/or behaviors that support the accomplishments and areas of improvement cited.

5. No Surprises

This isn't a birthday party; it's a performance appraisal. It should be pre-scheduled, held in a private location for a set period of time and focused on defined goals. Typically you and your manager have been meeting periodically prior to this appraisal, so the information contained in your appraisal shouldn't be shocking.

6. Clear Direction

At the end of your performance review, you should leave with a clear action plan, including understandable goals for your next performance appraisal, specific ways to measure your goals, how to modify any areas of improvement and the timing of your next performance appraisal.

You made it through your 90-day appraisal, and you're on your way to a successful new career with your company. Congratulations. I wish you the best of luck with this and all of your future endeavors!

Chapter Nine | After You Land | The First 90 Days | Review

Chapter 9.1 | Before Day One

- Celebrate your success.
- The week before day one, test-drive your commute, eat well, start a new sleeping schedule.
- Two nights before day one, head to bed early.
- The night before day one, lay out your clothes, set two alarms, go to bed early and avoid sleep aids.

Chapter 9.2 | Your First 30 Days

- Day one success tips: arrive 10 minutes early, pack protein snacks, speak up.
- It takes 21 days to develop a habit, so eat well, sleep well and exercise to power through your first 30 days.
- Get a mentor, be on time all the time, show results.
- Be observant and start strong.
- Work with your manager to set goals you C.A.R.E. about.

Chapter 9.3 | "The Comfort Zone" Days 31-90

- Smart scheduling means you arrive early, stay late and you're productive.
- Avoid lunchtime traps.
- Dress to impress: dress for the job you want, not the one you have.

Chapter 9.4 | 90 Day Performance Appraisal

- Your appraisal meeting should last about 30 minutes to one hour.

- You're in great shape with C.A.R.E. goals set in the first 30 days.
- Prepare for all types of feedback: the good and the ugly.
- Listen for ways to improve your performance. Learn.
- Regular meetings with your manager will ensure zero surprises.
- Get clear direction, set new/different goals and set your next appraisal date.

It's over, You did it. I'm proud of you and more importantly, you should be proud of you too. I would love to hear about your journey through the 9 Ways to Win the Job Search Game. Please send me your story by contacting me at www.adrianallames.com

ADDING IT UP

CAREER SUDOKU QUIZ

"Beginner minds see many options, but to experts there are but a few."
- Zen Buddhist

Ready to test your skills? Take this short 10-question quiz to find out your *Career Sudoku* score.

1. What three components do you need for a résumé that gets results?
    a. Focus on results, check spelling with human eyes and at least three pages
    b. Layout counts, two pages 85% of the time and triple spell-check
    c. Always one page, auto spell-check and results on bottom half

2. When it comes to personal branding, how long should your powerful 30-second pitch be?
   a. 15 words or less and within 15 seconds
   b. Under 60 seconds
   c. 30 seconds

3. Interviewing questions are important for:
   a. The interviewer and the interviewee
   b. The interviewer only
   c. The interviewer and recruiter only

4. Sending résumés and cover letters to job postings will land you interviews.
   a. True
   b. False

5. Phone interviews don't require thank-you notes.
   a. True
   b. False

6. Networking is about asking someone for a job.
   a. True
   b. False

7. Having dinner with friends can turn into a networking situation and job lead.
   a. True
   b. False

8. Your powerful 30-second pitch is also the answer to the #1 toughest interview question.
   a. True
   b. False

9. Arriving 20 minutes early to an interview is a good idea.

    a. True

    b. False

10. It's okay to take long lunches after the first week on the job.

    a. True

    b. False

Networking Resources Appendix

AARP, American Association for Retired Persons

AARP offers seminars on post-career planning and workforce re-entry. The seminars provide information and networking opportunities. To learn more, call the national headquarters at 800.424.3410.

AfricamVillage

10 W. Ashmead Place S.

Philadelphia, PA 19144

Phone: 215.848.0852

E-mail: yourhost@africamvillage.com

This Website features an Afrocentric mall, a development center and online networking.

African American Business Link

This directory and communication center for African American-owned businesses and organizations offers business links, online shopping, an employment center and a news magazine.

African Grapevine, Inc.

This community-based organization focuses on building financial wealth in the black community, networking, community services and markets, and professional development.

Black Career Women

P.O. Box 19332

Cincinnati, OH 45219

This is a national, professional development organization.

Black Voices: Black Wall Chat and Message Boards

This is a place to get your e-mail account, join chat clubs, go to message boards, and search the membership.

Graduate Degrees for Minorities (GEM) in Engineering and Science

GEM's mission is to enhance the human capital in engineering and science by increasing the participation of underrepresented minorities in graduate education through an array of services, including fellowships for education.

HACE

This organization provides links, services, programs and access for Hispanic professionals to private and public organizations, thereby strengthening the foundation for the professional and economic advancement of the Hispanic community.

HispanicBusiness.com

Associated with *Hispanic Business* magazine, this site offers networking events to the Hispanic community.

Hispanic Online

An online forum for Latinos living in the U.S., this site offers chat rooms, message boards, and news, events, and issues of interest to the Latino community.

International Society of African Scientists

P.O. Box 9209

Wilmington, DE 19809

This organization promotes the advancement of science and technology among people of African descent.

Multicultural Advantage Career Center

This is a complete career and job site for minority professionals and includes a job bank, career and job-hunting e-zines, diversity recruitment resources, support groups and chats, and links to minority professional associations.

National Association of Asian American Professionals

c/o NAAAP Chicago

P.O. Box 81138

Chicago, IL 60681

Hotline: 773.918.2454

E-mail: naaap@naaap.org

This national network of metropolitan organizations is dedicated to serving the needs of Asian American professionals across the U.S. and promotes Pan-Asian unity through fellowship and professional networking.

National Association of Negro Business and Professional Women's Clubs, Inc. (NANBPWC)
1806 New Hampshire Ave., NW
Washington, D.C. 20009
Phone: 202.483.4206
NANBPWC offers a job line, economic-development opportunities and community service projects.

National Black MBA Association, Inc.
180 N. Michigan Ave., Suite 1400
Chicago, IL 60601
Phone: 312.236.BMBA (2622)
FAX: 312.236.4131
E-mail: mail@nbmbaa.org
This business organization works to create economic and intellectual wealth for the black community.

National Society of Black Engineers
Membership, conventions, career fairs, pre-college activities and other helpful programs are sponsored by the NSBE.

National Society of Hispanic MBAs
8204 Elmbrook, Suite 235
Dallas, TX 75247
Toll-free phone: 877.467.4622
FAX: 214.267.1626
E-mail: info@nshmba.org
www.nshmba.org
Provides career networking opportunities for Hispanic business professionals.

Native Web Community Center

This Website's purpose is to bring together indigenous people from around the world by providing the tools and resources needed to communicate. It lists news, events, jobs and other community oriented resources. E-mail lists (with archives), chat boards, and more are planned for the future.

Nemnet

This resource organization is committed to helping minority students looking for jobs in education. Services include online job postings, résumé database, and career fairs for people of color. Free to job seekers.

UrbanExecs.com

This online networking resource targets young, affluent minority professionals. The site's mission is to enable upwardly mobile professionals to network, research career and educational opportunities, discuss business ventures and establish new ways to uplift urban America. Free to job seekers.

Journal Pages | Your Built-In Job Search Notebook

Adding It Up | Career Sudoku Quiz Answer Guide

1. What three components do you need for a résumé that gets results?
   a. Focus on results, check spelling with human eyes and at least three pages
   b. Layout counts, two pages 85% of the time and triple spell-check
   c. Always one page, auto spell-check and results on bottom half

2. When it comes to personal branding, how long should your powerful 30-second pitch be?
   a. 15 words or less and within 15 seconds
   b. Under 60 seconds
   c. 30 seconds

3. Interviewing questions are important for:
   a. The interviewer and the interviewee
   b. The interviewer only
   c. The interviewer and recruiter only

4. Sending résumés and cover letters to job postings will land you interviews.
   a. True
   b. False

5. Phone interviews don't require thank-you notes.
   a. True
   b. False

6. Networking is about asking someone for a job.
   a. True
   b. False

7. Having dinner with friends can turn into a networking situation and job lead.
   a. True
   b. False

8. Your powerful 30-second pitch is also the answer to the #1 toughest interview question.
   a. True
   b. False

9. Arriving 20 minutes early to an interview is a good idea.
   a. True
   b. False

10. It's okay to take long lunches after the first week on the job.
    a. True
    b. False

Made in the USA
Charleston, SC
21 July 2010